BIBLE STORIES · FOR YOUNG ONES ·

WOMEN OF COURAGE

*A read-along storybook on
great women of the Bible*

THOMAS NELSON PUBLISHERS
Nashville

The following selections from the Bible describe the lives of women who exhibited the quality of courage. Not that the Bible is a book of heroes; these women were human beings like us, who needed the strength that only God can give, and only to those who trust him. The example is theirs, but the glory is his.

The Bible used is the Contemporary English Version, an accurate translation of the original texts into clear, natural, current English that readers of all ages can understand and enjoy.

The stories are illustrated by beautiful watercolor paintings by artist Natalie Carabetta.

Whether they are being read to or are reading the stories themselves, children will be delighted with the vivid narration of these women's lives, as they learn what God can do when we put our faith in him.

Difficult phrases or passages are marked with a star (*) and are explained in *Notes* in the back of the book, where they are listed by page numbers.

CONTENTS

❖ —— Sarah —— ❖

This is the story of a great lady who at first lived in Ur with her husband Abraham. Ur was an important city in the country we today call Iraq. Sarah means "princess" and Abraham means "father of many peoples." The original names of this couple were Abram and Sarai. As we continue to follow the lives of the members of this family, we will see that Sarah was a woman of true courage.

(Genesis 11.26-32)

After Terah was seventy years old, he had three sons: Abram, Nahor, and Haran, who became the father of Lot. Terah's sons were born in the city of Ur in Chaldea,* and Haran died there before the death of his father. This is the story of Terah's descendants.

Abram married Sarai, but she was not able to have any children. And Nahor married Milcah, who was the daughter of Haran and the sister of Iscah.

Terah decided to move from Ur to the land of Canaan. He took along Abram and Sarai and his grandson Lot, the son of Haran. But when they came to the city of Haran,* they settled there. Terah lived to be two hundred five years old and died in Haran.

When Terah died, something happened to Abram and Sarai that would change their lives forever.

(Genesis 12.1-5)

The LORD said to Abram:

Leave your country, your family, and your relatives and go to the land that I will show you. I will bless you and make your descendants into a great nation. You will become famous and be a

blessing to others. I will bless anyone who says good things about you, but I will put a curse on anyone who says evil things about you. Everyone on earth will be blessed because of you.

Abram was seventy-five years old when the LORD told him to leave the city of Haran. He obeyed and left with his nephew Lot, his wife Sarai, and all the possessions and slaves they had gotten while in Haran.

Sarai had made a home in Haran. First she had left her familiar surroundings in Ur. Now she would again have to move with her husband to a strange new country. Also, Abram was already 75 years old and Sarai was 65. But she believed the wonderful promises of God and came gladly to Canaan with her husband, with his nephew, and the others who were with them.

The land of Canaan is called Palestine today. There Abram was a stranger and a wanderer, moving from place to place with no certain home. But he and Sarah still believed God's promise that someday this land would belong to their descendants, and they would be the father and mother of many nations.

(Genesis 17.1-8)

Abram was ninety-nine years old when the LORD appeared to him again and said, "I am God All-Powerful. If you obey me and always do right, I will keep my promise to you and give you more descendants than can be counted." Abram bowed with his face to the ground, and God said:

I promise that you will be the father of many nations. That's why I now change your name from Abram to Abraham.* I will give you a lot of descendants, and in the future they will become great nations. Some of them will even be kings.

I will always keep the solemn promise I have made to you and your descendants, because I am your God and their God. I will give you and them the land in which you are now a foreigner. I will give the whole land of Canaan to your family forever, and I will be their God.

(Genesis 17.15-22)

Abraham, from now on, your wife's name will be Sarah instead of Sarai. I will bless her, and you will have a son by her. She will become the mother of nations, and some of her descendants will even be kings.

Abraham bowed with his face to the ground and thought, "I am almost a hundred years old. How can I become a father? And Sarah is ninety. How can she have a child?" So he started laughing. Then he asked God, "Why not let Ishmael* inherit what you have promised me?"

But God answered:

No! You and Sarah will have a son, whose name will be Isaac,* and I will make an everlasting promise to him and his descendants.

I have heard what you have asked me to do for Ishmael, and so I will also bless him with many descendants. He will be the father of twelve princes, and I will make his family a great nation. But your son Isaac will be born about this time next year, and the promise I am making to you and your family will be for him and his descendants forever.

God finished speaking to Abraham and then left.

Sarah and Abraham (as God had now named them) were greatly puzzled by the Lord's announcement. Abraham had another son, Ishmael. So Abraham wondered why Ishmael couldn't be allowed to fulfill the promises God had made. Besides the couple was surely too old now to have children, so how was Sarah to have a baby? She would have to patiently wait and see what God was going to do.

(Genesis 18.1-15)

One hot summer afternoon Abraham was sitting by the entrance to his tent near the sacred trees of Mamre, when the LORD appeared to him. Abraham looked up and saw three men standing nearby. He quickly ran to meet them, bowed with his face to the ground, and said, "Please

come to my home where I can serve you. I'll have some water brought, so you can wash your feet, then you can rest under the tree. Let me get you some food to give you strength before you leave. I would be honored to serve you."

"Thank you very much," they answered. "We accept your offer."

Abraham quickly went to his tent and said to Sarah, "Hurry! Get a large sack of flour and make some bread." After saying this, he rushed off to his herd of cattle and picked out one of the best calves, which his servant quickly prepared. He served his guests some yogurt and milk, together with the meat.

While they were eating, he stood near them under the trees, and they asked him, "Where is your wife Sarah?"

"She is right there in the tent," Abraham answered.

One of the guests was the LORD, and he said, "I'll come back next spring, and when I do, Sarah will already have a son."

Sarah was behind him, listening at the entrance to the tent. Abraham and Sarah were very old, and Sarah was past the age for having children. So she laughed and said to herself, "Now that I am worn out and my husband is old, will I really know such happiness?"*

The LORD said to Abraham, "Why did Sarah laugh and doubt that she could have a child in her old age? I am the LORD! There is nothing too difficult for me. I'll come back next year at the time I said I would, and Sarah will already have a son."

Sarah was frightened. So she lied and said, "I didn't laugh."

"Yes, you did!" he answered.

All this seemed like a funny story to Sarah. But God wasn't angry with her.

(Genesis 21.1-7)

The LORD was good to Sarah and kept his promise. Although Abraham was very old, Sarah had a son at the

time God had said she would. Abraham named his son Isaac, and when the boy was eight days old, Abraham circumcised him, just as the LORD had commanded.

Abraham was a hundred years old when Isaac was born, and Sarah said, "God has made me laugh!* Now everyone will laugh with me. Who would have dared tell Abraham that someday I would have a child? But in his old age, I have given him a son."

❖——— **Hagar** ———❖

God had promised Abram and Sarai a family. But it was hard for them to wait patiently for it.

(Genesis 16.1-16)

Abram's wife Sarai had not been able to have any children. But she owned a young Egyptian slave woman named Hagar, and Sarai said to Abram, "The LORD has not given me any children. Sleep with my slave, and if she has a child, it will be mine."* Abram agreed, and Sarai gave him Hagar to be his wife. This happened after Abram had lived in the land of Canaan for ten years. Later, when Hagar knew she was going to have a baby, she became proud and was hateful to Sarai.

Then Sarai said to Abram, "It's all your fault! I gave you my slave woman, but she has been hateful to me ever since she found out she was going to have a baby. You have done me wrong, and you will have to answer to the LORD for this."

Abram said, "All right! She's your slave, and you can do whatever you want with her." After that, Sarai treated Hagar so mean that she finally ran away.

Hagar stopped to rest at a spring in the desert on the road to Shur. While she was there, the angel of the LORD came to her and asked, "Hagar, where have you come from, and where are you going?"

She answered, "I'm running away from Sarai, my owner."

The angel said, "Go back to Sarai and be her slave. I will give you a son, whose name will be Ishmael,* because I have heard your cry for help. And later I will give you so many descendants that no one will be able to count them all. But your son will be like a wild donkey, fighting everyone, and everyone fighting him. He will live far from all his relatives."

Hagar thought, "Have I really seen God and lived to tell about it?" So from then on she called him, "The God Who Sees Me."* That's why people call the well between Kadesh and Bered, "The Well of the Living One Who Sees Me."

Abram was eighty-six years old when Hagar gave birth to their son, and he named him Ishmael.

The name Ishmael means "God hears."

Years later, Sarah did give birth to Isaac, the son God had promised earlier. His name means "laughter," and his parents were now glad for this name because of the joy their son brought them.

(Genesis 21.8-21)

The time came when Sarah no longer had to nurse Isaac,* and on that day, Abraham gave a great banquet for his friends.

Hagar's son Ishmael was there, and Sarah saw him playing.* Sarah told Abraham, "Get rid of that Egyptian slave woman and her son! I don't want him to inherit anything. It should all go to my son."*

Abraham was worried about Ishmael. But God said,

"Abraham, don't worry about your slave woman and the
boy. Just do what Sarah tells you. Isaac will inherit your
family name, but the son of the slave woman is also your
son, and I will make his family into a nation."

Early the next morning, Abraham put an animal skin
full of water on Hagar's shoulder and gave her some bread.
Then he sent Hagar and her son away, and they wandered
around in the desert near Beersheba.

After they had run out of water, Hagar put her son
under a bush. Then she sat down a long way off, because
she could not bear to watch him die. And she cried bitterly.

When God heard the boy crying, the angel of God
called out to Hagar from heaven and said, "Hagar, why are
you worried? Don't be afraid. I have heard your son crying.

Help him up and hold his hand, because I will make him the father of a great nation." Then God let her see a well. So she went to the well, filled the skin with water, and gave some to her son.

God blessed Ishmael, and as the boy grew older, he became an expert with his bow and arrows. He lived in Paran Desert, and his mother chose an Egyptian woman for him to marry.

❖ ── Rebekah ── ❖

Abraham and Sarah were given one son, Isaac. But God had promised them a large family that would bless the whole world. How would this happen?

(Genesis 24.1-67)

Abraham was now a very old man. The LORD had made him rich, and he was successful in everything he did. One day, Abraham called in his oldest servant, who was in charge of all that he owned. Abraham told him, "Solemnly promise me in the name of the LORD, who rules heaven and earth, that you won't choose a wife for my son Isaac from the people here in the land of Canaan. Instead, go back to the land where I was born and find a wife for him from among my relatives."

But the servant asked, "What if the young woman I choose refuses to leave home and come here with me? Should I send Isaac there to look for a wife?"

"No!" Abraham answered. "Don't ever do that, no matter what! The LORD who rules heaven brought me here from the land of my birth and promised that he would give this land to my descendants forever. When you go back there, the LORD will send his angel ahead of you to help you find a wife for my son. If the young woman refuses to come along, you don't have to keep this promise. But don't ever take my son back there." So the servant gave Abraham his word that he would do everything he had been told to do.

Soon after that, the servant loaded ten of Abraham's camels with valuable gifts. Then he set out for the city in Mesopotamia where Abraham's brother Nahor lived.

When he got there, he let the camels rest near the well outside the city. It was late afternoon, the time when the women came there for water. The servant prayed:

You, LORD, are the God my master Abraham worships. Please keep your promise to him and let me find a wife for Isaac today. The young women of the city will soon come to this well for water, and I'll ask one of them for a drink. If she gives me a drink and then offers to get some water for my camels, I'll know she is the one you have chosen and that you have kept your promise to my master.

While he was still praying, a young and beautiful unmarried woman came by with a water jar on her shoulder. She was Rebekah, the daughter of Bethuel, the son of Abraham's brother Nahor and his wife Milcah. Rebekah walked past Abraham's servant, went over to the well, and filled her water jar. When she started back, Abraham's servant ran to her and said, "Please let me have a drink of water!"

"Sir, I'll be glad to," she answered. Then she quickly took the jar from her shoulder and held it while he drank. After he had finished, she said, "Now I'll give your camels all the water they want." She quickly poured out water for them, and she kept going back for more, until his camels had drunk all they wanted. Abraham's servant did not say a word, but he watched everything Rebekah did, because he

wanted to know if this was the young woman the LORD had chosen.

The servant had brought along an expensive gold ring and two large gold bracelets. When Rebekah had finished bringing the water, he put the ring in her nose* and the bracelets on her arm. Then he said, "Please tell me who your father is. Does he have room in his house for me and my men to spend the night?"

She answered, "My father is Bethuel, the son of Nahor and Milcah. We have a place where you and your men can stay, and we also have straw and feed for your camels."

Then the servant got down on his knees and prayed, "I thank you, LORD God of my master Abraham! You have led me to his relatives and kept your promise to him, just as you said you would."

Rebekah ran straight home and told her family everything. Her brother Laban heard her tell what the servant had said, and he saw the ring and the bracelets she was wearing. So he ran out to Abraham's servant, who was standing by his camels at the well. He said to the servant, "The LORD has brought you safely here! Come home with me. There's no need for you to keep on standing outside. I have a room ready for you in my house, and there is also a place for your camels."

Abraham's servant went home with Laban, where Laban's servants unloaded his camels and gave them straw and feed. Then they brought water into the house, so Abraham's servant and his men could wash their feet. After that, they brought in food. But the servant said, "Before I eat, I must tell you why I have come."

"Go ahead, tell us," Laban answered.

The servant explained:

I am Abraham's servant. The LORD has been good to my master and has made him very rich. God has given him many sheep, goats, cattle, camels, and donkeys, as well as a lot of silver and gold, and many slaves. Sarah, my master's wife, didn't have any children until she was very old. Then she had a son, and my master has given him everything. I solemnly promised my master that I would do what he said. And he told me, "Don't choose a wife for my son from the women in the land of Canaan. Instead, go back to the land I came from and find a wife for my son from among my relatives."

I asked my master, "What if the young woman refuses to come with me?"

My master answered, "I have always obeyed the LORD, and he will send his angel to help you find a wife for my son from my own relatives. But if they refuse to let her come back with you, then you no longer have to keep your promise."

When I came to the well today, I silently prayed, "You, LORD, are the God my master Abraham worships, so please lead me to a wife for his son while I am here at the well. When a young woman comes out to get water, I'll ask her to give me a drink. If she gives me a drink and offers to get some water for my camels, I'll know she is the one you have chosen."

Even before I had finished praying, Rebekah came by with a water jar on her shoulder. When she

had filled her jar, I asked her for a drink. She quickly lowered the jar from her shoulder and said, "Have a drink. Then I'll get water for your camels." So I drank, and after that she got some water for my camels. I asked her who her father was, and she answered, "My father is Bethuel the son of Nahor and Milcah." Right away I put the ring in her nose and the bracelets on her arms. Then I got down on my knees and gave thanks to the God my master Abraham worships. The LORD had led me straight to my master's relatives, and I had found a wife for his son.

Now please tell me if you are willing to do the right thing for my master. Will you treat him fairly, or do I have to look for another young woman?"

Laban and Bethuel answered, "The LORD has done this! We have no choice in the matter. Take Rebekah with you, and let her marry your master's son, just as the LORD has said." Abraham's servant bowed down and gave thanks to the LORD. Then he unpacked clothes, as well as silver and gold jewelry, and gave it all to Rebekah. He also gave expensive gifts to her brother and her mother.

Abraham's servant and the men with him ate and drank, then they spent the night there. The next morning, they got up, and the servant told Rebekah's mother and brother, "I would like to go back to my master now."

"Let Rebekah stay with us for a week or ten days," they answered. "Then she may go."

But he said, "Don't make me stay any longer. The LORD has helped me find a wife for my master's son. Now let us return."

They answered, "Let's ask Rebekah what she wants to do." They called her and asked, "Are you willing to leave with this man right now?"

"Yes!" she answered.

So they decided to let Rebekah and an old family servant woman* leave immediately with Abraham's servant and his men. They gave Rebekah their blessing, and said, "We pray that God will give you many children and grandchildren and that he will let them defeat their enemies." Afterwards, Rebekah and the young women who were to travel with her prepared to leave. Then they got on camels and left with Abraham's servant and his men.

At that time, Isaac was living in the southern part of Canaan near a place called "The Well of the Living One Who Sees Me."* One evening he went walking in the fields, when suddenly he saw some people coming on camels. So he started toward them. Rebekah saw him coming, got down from her camel, and asked, "Who is that man?"

"He is my master Isaac," the servant answered. Then she covered her face with her veil.*

The servant told Isaac everything that had happened.

Isaac took Rebekah into the tent* where his mother had lived before she died, and Rebekah became his wife. He loved her and was comforted over the loss of his mother.

(Genesis 25.20-28)

Isaac was forty years old when he married Rebekah, who was the daughter of Bethuel and the sister of Laban, the Aramean from Paddan Aram.*

Almost twenty years later, Rebekah still had no children. So Isaac asked the LORD to let her have a child, and the LORD answered his prayer.

Before Rebekah gave birth, she knew she was going to have twins, because she could feel them inside her, fighting each other. She thought, "If I had known it was going to be like this, I wouldn't have wanted a baby." Finally, she asked the LORD why her twins were fighting, and he told her:

> "Your two sons
> will become two nations
>   always at war.
> The younger of the two
>   will be stronger,
> and the older son
>   will be his servant."

When Rebekah gave birth, the first baby was covered all over with red hair, so he was named Esau.* The second baby grabbed on to his brother's heel, so they named him Jacob.* Isaac was sixty years old when they were born.

As Jacob and Esau grew older, Esau liked the outdoors and became a good hunter, while Jacob settled down and became a shepherd. Esau would take the meat of wild animals to his father Isaac, and so Isaac loved him best, but Jacob was his mother's favorite son.

So Rebekah did a very bold thing for the son she loved.

(Genesis 27.1-46)

After Isaac had become old and blind, he called in his first-born son Esau, who asked him, "Father, what can I do for you?"

Isaac replied, "I am old and might die at any time. So take your bow and arrows, go out in the fields, and kill a wild animal. Cook some of that tasty food that I love so much and bring it to me. I want to eat it once more and give you my blessing before I die."

Rebekah had been listening, and as soon as Esau left to go hunting, she said to Jacob, "I heard your father tell Esau to kill a wild animal and cook him some tasty food, because before your father dies, he wants to bless your brother with the LORD as his witness. Now, son, listen carefully to what I want you to do. Go and kill two of your best young goats and bring them to me. I'll cook the tasty food that your father loves so much. Then you can take it to him, so he can eat it and give you his blessing before he dies."

"My brother Esau is a hairy man," Jacob reminded her. "And I am not. If my father touches me and thinks I am trying to trick him, he'll put a curse on me instead of giving me a blessing."

Rebekah insisted, "Let his curse fall on me! Just do what I say and bring me the meat." So Jacob brought the meat to his mother, and she cooked the tasty food that his father liked. Then she took some of Esau's best clothes and put them on Jacob. She also covered the smooth part of his hands and neck with the goatskins and gave him some bread and the tasty food she had cooked.

Jacob went to his father and said, "Father, here I am."

"Which one of my sons are you?" his father asked.

Jacob replied, "I am Esau, your first-born son, and I have done what you told me to do. Now please sit up and eat the meat I have brought. Then you can give me your blessing."

Isaac asked, "My son, how did you find an animal so quickly?"

"The LORD your God was kind to me," Jacob answered.

"My son," Isaac said, "come closer, where I can touch you and find out if you really are Esau." Jacob went closer. His father touched him and said, "You sound like Jacob, but your hands feel hairy like Esau's." And so Isaac blessed Jacob, thinking he was Esau.

Isaac asked, "Are you really my son Esau?"

"Yes, I am!" Jacob answered.

So Isaac told him, "Serve me the wild meat, and I can give you my blessing."

Jacob gave him some meat, and he ate it. He also gave him some wine, and he drank it. Then Isaac said, "Son, come over here and kiss me." While Jacob was kissing him, Isaac smelled his clothes and said:

"The smell of my son
is like a field
the LORD has blessed!
God will bless you, my son,
with dew from heaven
and with fertile fields,
rich with grain and grapes.
Nations will be your servants
and bow down to you.
You will rule your brothers,
and they will kneel
at your feet.
Anyone who curses you
will be cursed;
anyone who blesses you
will be blessed!"

Right after Isaac had given Jacob his blessing and Jacob had gone, Esau came back from hunting. He cooked the tasty food, brought it to his father, and said, "Father, please sit up and eat the meat I have brought you, so you can give me your blessing."

"Who are you?" Isaac asked.

"I am Esau, your first-born son."

Isaac started trembling and said, "Then who brought me some wild meat right before you came in? I ate it and gave him a blessing that cannot be taken back."

Esau cried loudly and begged, "Father, give me a blessing too!"

Isaac answered, "Your brother tricked me and stole your blessing."

Esau replied, "My brother deserves the name Jacob,* because he has already cheated me twice. The first time he cheated me out of my rights as the first-born son, and now he has cheated me out of my blessing." Then Esau asked his father, "Don't you still have a blessing for me?"

"Son," Isaac answered, "I have made Jacob ruler over you and your brothers, and all of you are to be his servants. I have also promised him all the grain and grapes that he needs. What else is left for me to do for you?"

"Father," Esau asked, "don't you have more than one blessing? You can surely give me a blessing too?" Then Esau started crying again.

So his father said:

"Your home will be far
from the fertile land,
where dew comes down
from the heavens.
You will live by the power
of your sword
and be your brother's slave.
But when you decide to be free,
you will break loose."

Esau hated Jacob because he had been given the blessing from their father. So he said to himself, "Just as soon as my father dies, I'll kill Jacob."

When Rebekah found out what Esau planned to do, she sent for Jacob and told him, "Son, your brother Esau is just waiting for the time when he can kill you. Now listen carefully and do what I say. Go to the home of my brother Laban in Haran and stay with him for a while. When your brother stops being angry and forgets what you have done to him, I'll send for you to come home. Why should I lose both of my sons on the same day?"*

Rebekah told Isaac, "Those Hittite wives of Esau are making my life miserable! If Jacob marries a Hittite woman, I'd be better off dead."

Rebekah and Jacob were wrong to deceive Isaac. The family was forced apart by their dishonesty. Although Jacob was his mother's favorite, he would not be with her much longer.

(Genesis 28.1-5)

Isaac called in Jacob, gave him his blessing, and said:
Don't marry any of those Canaanite women!
Go at once to your mother's father Bethuel in Paddan Aram* and choose a wife from one of the daughters of Laban, your mother's brother. I pray that God All-Powerful will bless you with many descendants and let you become a great nation. May he bless you with the land he gave Abraham, so that you will take over this land where we now live as foreigners.

Isaac then sent Jacob to Paddan Aram to stay with Rebekah's brother Laban, the son of Bethuel the Aramean.

After this, Jacob had a face-to-face meeting with God one day. Jacob's life was completely changed, and God called him and his descendants Israel, meaning "prince with God." Rebekah's hopes for her favorite son were at last fulfilled— but not in the way she had planned.

❖ —— Miriam —— ❖

This story is about Miriam, a young girl in the nation of Israel who rescued her baby brother Moses, the one who would be her people's greatest leader.

You remember Jacob. He had twelve sons. Ten of the older sons became jealous of their young brother Joseph, so they sold him to be a slave in Egypt. But later Joseph became a famous government official in that land. When his family was suffering from a famine in Canaan, Joseph brought them all to live in Egypt where he cared for them during the rest of his life.

(Exodus 1.8-22)

Many years after the death of Joseph,* a new king came to power in Egypt. This king did not know anything about Joseph, and he told the Egyptians:

> There are too many of those Israelites in our country, and they are more powerful than we are. If we don't outsmart them, there will be more and more of them. And if our country goes to war, they could easily fight on the side of our enemies and leave Egypt.

The Egyptians put slave bosses in charge of the people of Israel and tried to wear them down with hard work. They forced them to build the cities of Pithom and Rameses,* where the king could store his supplies. But even though they were mistreated, their families grew larger, and they took over more land. Because of this, the Egyptians hated them even more and made them work so hard that their lives became miserable. The Egyptians were cruel to the people of Israel and forced them to make bricks and to mix mortar and to work in the fields.

Finally, the king called in Shiphrah and Puah, the two women who helped the Hebrew* mothers when they gave birth. He told them, "If a Hebrew woman gives birth to a girl, you can let the child live. If the baby is a boy, kill him!"

But the two women were faithful to God and did not kill the boys, even though the king had told them to. The king called them in again and asked, "Why are you letting those baby boys live?"

They answered, "Hebrew women have their babies much quicker than Egyptian women. By the time we get to them, their babies are already born."

God was good to the two women because they obeyed him. He let them get married and have families of their own. And there were also more Israelites than ever before. Finally, the king gave a command to everyone in the nation, "As soon as a Hebrew boy is born, throw him into the Nile River! But you can let the girls live."

(Exodus 2.1-10)

A man from the tribe of Levi married a woman from the same tribe, and she later had a baby boy. He was a

beautiful child, and she hid him for three months. But when she could no longer keep him hidden, she made a basket out of reeds and covered it with tar. She put him in the basket and placed it in the tall grass along the edge of the river. Miriam, the baby's older sister, stood off at a distance to see what would happen to him.

About that time the king's daughter came down to bathe in the river, while her servant women walked along the river bank. She saw the basket in the tall grass and sent one of the young women to pull it to the bank. When the king's daughter opened the basket, she saw the baby and felt sorry for him, because he was crying. She said, "This must be one of the Hebrew babies."

At once the baby's older sister came up and asked, "Do you want me to get one of the Hebrew women to take care of him for you?"

"Yes," the king's daughter said. So the girl brought the baby's mother, and the king's daughter told her, "Take care of this child, and I will pay you."

The baby's mother carried him home and took care of him. And when he was old enough, she took him to the king's daughter, who adopted him. She named him Moses,* because she said, "I pulled him out of the water."

So Moses became a prince in Egypt, and he finally led his own people Israel out of Egyptian slavery. The brave older sister who had watched over the baby Moses was Miriam. Moses and Miriam had another brother, Aaron, who became Moses' assistant.

(Exodus 15.20-21)

Years later, Miriam the sister of Aaron became a prophet. One day, she took her tambourine and led the

other women out to play their tambourines and to dance. Then she sang this song to them:

> Sing praises to the LORD
> for his great victory!
> He has thrown horses
> and chariot drivers
> into the sea.

Miriam had good reason to sing and dance. The baby brother she had saved from the Nile became her people's great rescuer and lawgiver.

❖ ── Rahab ── ❖

God often selected the most surprising people to be his heroes. One of these was Rahab, a woman in the town of Jericho.

(Joshua 2.1-21)

Joshua chose two men to be spies and told them, "Go across the river and find out as much as you can about the whole area, and especially about the town of Jericho."

The two spies left the Israelite camp at Acacia* and went to Jericho, where they decided to spend the night at the house of a woman* named Rahab.

But someone found out about them and told the king of Jericho, "Some Israelite men came here tonight. They are spies!" The king ordered some soldiers to go to Rahab's house and arrest the spies. Meanwhile, Rahab had taken the men up to the flat roof of her house and helped them hide under some piles of harvested flax plants* that she had put there to dry.

The soldiers came to her door and demanded, "Let us have the men who are staying at your house. They are spies!"

She answered, "Some men did come to my house, but I didn't know where they had come from. They left about sunset, just before it was time to close the town gate.* I don't know where they were going, but if you hurry, maybe you can catch them."

The guards at the town gate let the soldiers leave Jericho, but they closed the gate again as soon as the soldiers went through. Then the soldiers headed toward the Jordan River to look for the spies at the place where people cross the river.

Rahab went back up to her roof. The spies were still awake, so she told them:

> I know that the LORD has given you this land. Everyone shakes with fear because of you. We heard how the LORD dried up the Red Sea* so you could leave Egypt. And we heard how you destroyed Sihon

and Og, those two Amorite kings east of the Jordan River. We know that the LORD your God rules heaven and earth, and we've lost our courage and our will to fight back.

Please promise me in the LORD's name that you will be as kind to my family as I have been to you. Do something to show that you won't let your people kill my father and mother and my brothers and sisters and their families.

"Rahab," the spies answered, "if you keep quiet about what we're doing, we promise to be kind to you when the LORD gives us this land."

Rahab's house was built into the town wall,* and one of the windows in her house went through the wall. She gave the spies a rope, showed them the window, and said, "Use this rope to let yourselves down to the ground outside the wall. Then hide in the hills. The men who are looking for you won't be able to find you there. They'll give up and come back after a few days, and you can leave."

The spies said:

You made us promise to let you and your family live. We'll keep our promise, but you can't tell anyone why we were here. You must tie this red rope on your window when we attack, and your father and mother, your brothers, and everyone else in your family must be here with you. We'll take the blame if anyone inside this house gets hurt. But anyone who leaves your house will be killed, and it won't be our fault.

"I'll do exactly what you said," Rahab promised. Then she let them leave and tied the red rope to the window.

(Joshua 6.1-27)

Meanwhile, the people of Jericho had been keeping the gates in their town wall locked because they were afraid of the Israelites. No one could go out, and no one could get in.

The LORD said to Joshua:

> I will help you and your army defeat the king of Jericho and his army, and you will capture the town. Here is how to do it: March slowly around Jericho once a day for six days. Take along the sacred chest and have seven priests carry trumpets* and walk in front of it.
>
> On the seventh day, march slowly around the town seven times while the priests blow their trumpets. Then the priests will blast on their trumpets, and everyone else will shout. The town walls will fall down, and your soldiers can go straight into the town.

Joshua called the priests together and said, "Take the chest and have seven priests carry trumpets and march ahead of it."

Next he gave the army their orders: "March slowly around Jericho. A few of you will go ahead of the chest to guard it, but most of you will follow it. Don't shout the battle cry or yell or even talk until the day I tell you to. Then let out a shout!"

As soon as Joshua finished giving the orders, they started marching. One group of soldiers led the way, with seven priests marching behind them and blowing trumpets. Then came the priests carrying the chest, followed by all the other soldiers. They obeyed Joshua's orders and carried the chest once around the town before returning to camp for the night.

Early the next morning, Joshua and everyone else got up and set out to march around Jericho again. They were in the same order as the day before. One group of soldiers was in front, followed by the seven priests with trumpets and the priests who carried the chest. The rest of the army came last. The seven priests blew their trumpets as everyone marched slowly around Jericho and back to camp. They did this once a day for six days.

On the seventh day, the army got up at daybreak. They marched slowly around Jericho the same as they had done for six days, except on this day they went around seven times. Then the priests blew the trumpets, and Joshua yelled:

Get ready to shout! The LORD will let you capture this town. But you must destroy it and everything in it to show that it now belongs to the LORD.* Rahab helped the spies we sent,* so protect her and the others who are inside her house. But kill everyone else in the town. The silver and gold and everything made of bronze and iron belong to the LORD and must be put in his treasury. Be careful to follow these instructions, because if you see something you want and take it, God will destroy Israel! And it will be all your fault.*

The priests blew their trumpets again, and the soldiers shouted as loud as they could. The walls of Jericho fell flat! Then soldiers rushed up the hill, went straight into the town, and captured it. They killed everyone, men and women, young and old, everyone except Rahab and the others in her house. They even killed every cow, sheep, and donkey.

Joshua talked with the two men he had sent as spies. "Rahab kept you safe when I sent you to Jericho," Joshua said. "We promised to protect her and her family, and we will keep that promise. Now go into her house and bring them out."

The two men went into Rahab's house and brought her out, along with her father and mother, her brothers, and her relatives. Rahab and her family had to stay in a place just outside the Israelite army camp.* But later on they were allowed to live among the Israelites, and her descendants still do.

The Israelites took the silver and gold and the things made of bronze and iron and put them with the rest of the treasure that was kept at the LORD's house.* Finally, they set fire to Jericho and everything in it.

After Jericho was destroyed, Joshua warned the people, "Someday a man will rebuild Jericho, but the LORD will put a curse on him. His oldest son will die when he starts to build the town wall. And by the time he finishes the wall and puts gates in it, all his children will be dead."*

The LORD helped Joshua in everything he did, and Joshua was famous everywhere in Canaan.

Rahab had been God's key to Joshua's success. Not only that, but Rahab was honored by God to become an ancestor of Jesus, who would be born over a thousand years later.

❖ —— Deborah ——❖

Deborah, a Hebrew judge and prophetess, was a crafty lady. Barak, the commander of Israel's army, was afraid to go into battle against the Canaanites without her. So Deborah went with him and his ten thousand troops. When the time came, it was Deborah's encouragement that enabled Barak to fight and win the battle.

(Judges 4.1-24)

After the death of Ehud, the Israelites again started disobeying the LORD. So the LORD let the Canaanite king Jabin of Hazor take control of Israel. Sisera was the commander of Jabin's army, and he lived in Harosheth-Ha-Goiim. Jabin's army had nine hundred chariots covered with iron. For twenty years he made life miserable for the Israelites, until finally they begged the LORD for help.

Deborah the wife of Lappidoth was a prophet and a leader* of Israel during those days. She would sit under Deborah's Palm Tree between Ramah and Bethel in the hill country of Ephraim, where Israelites would come and ask her to settle their legal cases.

One day, Barak the son of Abinoam was in Kedesh in Naphtali, and Deborah sent someone to ask him to come and talk with her. When he arrived, she said:

> I have a message for you from the LORD God of Israel! You are to get together an army of ten thousand men from the Naphtali and Zebulun tribes and lead them to Mount Tabor. The LORD will trick Sisera into coming out to fight you at the Kishon River. Sisera will be leading King Jabin's army as usual, and they will have their chariots, but the LORD has promised to help you defeat them!

"I'm not going unless you go!" Barak told her.

"All right, I'll go!" she replied. "But I'm warning you that the LORD is going to let a woman defeat Sisera, and no one will honor you for winning the battle."

Deborah and Barak left for Kedesh, where Barak called together the troops from Zebulun and Naphtali. Ten thousand soldiers gathered there, and Barak led them out from Kedesh. Deborah went too.

About this time, Heber of the Kenite clan was living near the village of Oak in Zaanannim,* not far from Kedesh. The Kenites were descendants of Hobab, the father-in-law of Moses, but Heber had moved and set up his tents away from the rest of the clan.

When Sisera learned that Barak had led an army to Mount Tabor, he called his troops together and got all nine hundred iron-covered war chariots ready. Then he led his army from Harosheth-Ha-Goiim to the Kishon River.

Deborah shouted, "Barak, it's time to attack Sisera! Because today the LORD is going to help you defeat him. In fact, the LORD has already gone on ahead to fight for you."

Barak led his ten thousand troops down from Mount Tabor. And during the battle, the LORD confused Sisera, his chariot drivers, and his whole army. Everyone was so afraid of Barak and his army, that even Sisera jumped down from his chariot and tried to run away. Barak's forces went after Sisera's chariots and army as far as Harosheth-Ha-Goiim.

Sisera's entire army was wiped out! Only Sisera escaped. He ran to Heber's camp, because Heber and his family had a peace treaty with the king of Hazor. Sisera went to the tent that belonged to Jael, Heber's wife. She came out to greet him. "Come in, sir," she said. "Please come on in. Don't be afraid."

After they had gone inside, Sisera lay down, and Jael covered him with a blanket. "Could I have a little water?" he asked. "I'm thirsty."

Jael opened a leather bottle and poured him some milk, then she covered him back up.

"Stand there at the tent door," Sisera told her. "If someone comes by and asks if anyone is inside, tell them 'No.' "

Sisera was exhausted and soon fell fast asleep. Jael

took a hammer and drove a tent-peg through his head into the ground, and he died.

Meanwhile, Barak had been following Sisera, and Jael went out to meet him. "The man you're looking for is inside," she said. "Come on in, and I'll show him to you."

They went inside, and there was the dead Sisera stretched out with a tent-peg through his skull.

That same day, the Israelites defeated the Canaanite King Jabin, and his army was no longer powerful enough to attack the Israelites. Jabin grew weaker while the Israelites kept growing stronger; at last the Israelites destroyed him.

(Judges 5.1-31)

After the battle was over that day, Deborah and Barak sang this song:

> We praise you, LORD!
> Our soldiers volunteered,
>> ready to follow you.
> Listen, kings and rulers,
> while I sing for the LORD,
>> the God of Israel.

Our LORD, God of Israel,
when you came from Seir,
        where the Edomites live,
rain poured from the sky,
the earth trembled,
        and mountains shook.

In the time of Shamgar
        son of Anath,
and now again in Jael's time,
roads were too dangerous
        for caravans.
Travelers had to take
        the back roads,
and villagers couldn't work
        in their fields.*
Then Deborah* took command,
protecting Israel as a mother
        protects her children.

The Israelites worshiped
        other gods,
and the gates of their towns
        were then attacked.*
But they had no shields
        or spears to fight with.
I praise you, LORD,
        and I am grateful
for those leaders and soldiers
        who volunteered.

Listen, everyone!
Whether you ride a donkey

with a padded saddle
or have to walk.
Anyone who carries water*
to the animals will tell you,
    "The LORD has won victories,
    and so has Israel."

Then the LORD's people marched
    down to the town gates.
"Deborah, let's go," they said.
"Let's sing as we march.
    Barak, capture our enemies."

The LORD's people who were left
joined with their leaders
    and fought at my side.*
Troops came from Ephraim,
    where Amalekites once lived.
Others came from Benjamin;
officers and leaders came
    from Machir and Zebulun.
The rulers of Issachar
    came along with Deborah,
and Issachar followed Barak
    into the valley.

But the tribe of Reuben
    was no help at all!*
Reuben, why did you stay
    among your sheep pens?*
Was it to listen to shepherds
    whistling for their sheep?
No one could figure out
    why Reuben wouldn't come.*

The people of Gilead stayed
across the Jordan.
Why did the tribe of Dan
remain on their ships
and the tribe of Asher
stay along the coast
near the harbors?

But soldiers of Zebulun
and Naphtali
risked their lives
to attack the enemy.*
Canaanite kings fought us
at Taanach by the stream
near Megiddo*—
but they couldn't rob us
of our silver.
From their pathways in the sky
the stars* fought Sisera,
and his soldiers were swept away
by the ancient Kishon River.

I will march on and be brave.

Sisera's horses galloped off,
their hoofs thundering
in retreat.

The LORD's angel said,
"Put a curse on Meroz Town!
Its people refused
to help the LORD fight
his powerful enemies."
But honor Jael,

the wife of Heber
        from the Kenite clan.
Give more honor to her
than to any other woman
        who lives in tents.
Yes, give more honor to her
        than to any other woman.
Sisera asked for water,
but Jael gave him milk —
        cream in a fancy cup.
She reached for a tent peg
and held a hammer
        in her right hand.
And with a blow to the head
        she crushed his skull.
Sisera sank to his knees
        and fell dead at her feet.

Sisera's mother looked out
        through her window.
"Why is he taking so long?"
        she asked.
"Why haven't we heard
        his chariots coming?"
She and her wisest women
        all gave the same answer:
"Sisera and his troops
are finding treasures
        to bring back —
a woman, or maybe two,
        for each man,
and beautiful dresses
        for those women to wear."*

Our LORD, we pray
that all your enemies
        will die like Sisera.
But let everyone who loves you
shine brightly
        like the sun at dawn.
There was peace in Israel for about forty years.

❖ —— Ruth —— ❖

*Ruth of Moab is one of history's great women of courage. The
people of Moab, across the Jordan River, were greatly hated
by Israel in ancient times. No one from Moab was allowed to
live in Israel. So it was also very unusual when a family
from Israel actually went to live in Moab—and their two
sons even married Moabite girls! When her Israelite
husband died, Ruth, one of the Moabite girls, decided to go
back to Israel with her mother-in-law, Naomi, who was now
also a widow. The younger woman's stubborn love finally
won the hearts of her mother-in-law's people.*

Ruth Is Loyal to Naomi

(Ruth 1.1-22)

Before Israel was ruled by kings, Elimelech from the
tribe of Ephrath lived in the town of Bethlehem. His wife
was named Naomi, and their two sons were Mahlon and
Chilion. But when crops failed, they moved to the country of
Moab.* While they were there, Elimelech died, leaving
Naomi with only her two sons.

Later, Naomi's sons married Moab women. One was
named Orpah and the other Ruth. About ten years later
Mahlon and Chilion also died. Now Naomi had no husband
or sons.

When Naomi heard that the LORD had given his people a good harvest, she and her two daughters-in-law got ready to leave Moab and go to Judah. As they were walking down the road, Naomi said to them, "Don't you want to go back home to your own mothers? You were kind to my husband and sons, and you have always been kind to me. I pray that the LORD will be just as kind to you. May he give each of you another husband."

Naomi kissed them. They cried and said, "We want to go with you and live among your people."

But she replied, "My daughters, why don't you return home? What good will it do you to go with me? Do you think I could have more sons for you to marry?* You must go back home, because I am too old to marry again. Even if I got married tonight and later had more sons, would you wait for them to become old enough to marry? No, my daughters! Life is harder for me than it is for you, because the LORD has turned against me."*

They cried again. Orpah kissed her mother-in-law good-by, but Ruth held on to her. Naomi then said to Ruth, "Look, your sister-in-law is going back to her people and to her gods! Why don't you go with her?"

Ruth answered,
        "Please don't tell me
        to leave you
                and return home!
        I will go where you go,
                I will live where you live;
        your people will be my people;
                your God will be my God.

I will die where you die
> and be buried beside you.
May the LORD punish me
if we are ever separated,
> even by death!"*

When Naomi saw that Ruth had made up her mind to go with her, she stopped urging her to go back.

They reached Bethlehem, and the whole town was excited to see them. The women who lived there asked, "Can this really be Naomi?"

Then she told them, "Don't call me Naomi any longer! Call me Mara,* because God has made my life bitter. I had everything when I left, but the LORD has brought me back with nothing. How can you still call me Naomi, when God has turned against me and made my life so hard?"

The barley harvest was just beginning when Naomi and her daughter-in-law came from Moab to Bethlehem.

Ruth Meets Boaz

(Ruth 2.1-23)

One day Ruth said to Naomi, "Let me see if I can find someone who will let me pick up the grain left in the fields by the harvest workers."*

Naomi answered, "Go ahead, my daughter." So right away Ruth went out to pick up grain in a field owned by Boaz. He was a relative of Naomi's husband Elimelech, as well as a rich and important man.

When Boaz left Bethlehem and went out to his field, he said to the harvest workers, "May the LORD be good to you!"

They replied, "And may the LORD bless you!"

Boaz asked the man in charge of the harvest workers, "Who is that young woman?"

The man answered, "She is the one who came back from Moab with Naomi. She asked if she could pick up grain left by the harvest workers, and she has been working all morning without a moment's rest."*

Boaz went over to Ruth and said, "Take my advice and don't pick up grain in anyone else's fields. Stay here with the women and follow along behind them, as they gather up what the men have cut. I have warned the men not to bother you, and whenever you are thirsty, you can drink from the water jars they have filled."

Ruth bowed down to the ground and said, "You know I come from another country. Why are you so good to me?"

Boaz answered, "I've heard how you've helped your mother-in-law ever since your husband died. You even left your own father and mother to come and live in a foreign land among people you don't know. I pray that the LORD God of Israel will reward you for what you have done. And now that you have come to him for help, I pray that he will be very kind to you."

Ruth replied, "Sir, it's good of you to speak kindly to me and make me feel so welcome. I'm not even one of your servants."

At mealtime Boaz said to Ruth, "Come, eat with us. Have some bread and dip it in the sauce." Right away she sat down with the workers, and Boaz handed her some roasted grain. Ruth ate all she wanted and had some left over.

When Ruth got up to go and pick up grain, Boaz told his men, "Don't stop her, even if she picks up grain from where it is stacked. Be sure to pull out some stalks of grain from the bundles and leave them on the ground for her. And don't bother her!"

Ruth worked in the field until evening. Then after

she had pounded the grain off the stalks, she had a large basket full of grain. She took the grain to town and showed Naomi how much she had picked up. Ruth also gave her the food left over from her lunch.

Naomi said, "Where did you work today? Whose field was it? God bless the man who treated you so well!" Then Ruth told her that she had worked in the field of a man named Boaz.

"May the LORD bless Boaz!" Naomi replied. "He* has shown that he is still loyal to the living and to the dead. Boaz is a close relative, one of those who is supposed to look after us."

Ruth told her, "He even said I could stay in the field with his workers until they had finished gathering all his grain."

Naomi replied, "My daughter, it's good that you can pick up grain alongside the women who work in his field. Who knows what might happen to you in someone else's field!" And so, Ruth stayed close to the women, while picking up grain in his field.

Ruth worked in the fields until the barley and wheat were harvested. And all this time she lived with Naomi.

Naomi Makes Plans for Ruth

(Ruth 3.1-18)

One day Naomi said to Ruth:

It's time I found you a husband, who will give you a home and take care of you.

You have been picking up grain alongside the women who work for Boaz, and you know he is a relative of ours. Tonight he will be threshing the grain. Now take a bath, put on some perfume, and dress up in your best clothes. Go where he is working, but don't let him see you until he has finished eating and drinking. Watch where he goes to spend the night, then when he is asleep, lift the covers and lie down at his feet.* He will tell you what to do.

Ruth answered, "I'll do whatever you say." She went out to the place where Boaz was working and did what Naomi had told her.

After Boaz finished eating and drinking and was feeling happy, he went over and fell asleep near the pile of grain. Ruth slipped over quietly. She lifted the covers and lay down near his feet.

In the middle of the night, Boaz suddenly woke up and was shocked to see a woman lying at his feet. "Who are you?" he asked.

"I am Ruth," she answered, "and you are the relative who is supposed to take care of me. So spread the edge of your cover over me."*

Boaz replied:

> May the LORD be good to you! This shows how truly loyal you are to your family. You could have looked for a younger man, either rich or poor, but you didn't. Don't worry, I'll do what you have asked. You are respected by everyone in town.

> It's true that I am one of the relatives who is supposed to take care of you, but there is someone who is an even closer relative. Stay here until morning, then I will find out if he is willing to look after you. If he isn't, I promise by the living God to do it myself. Now go back to sleep until morning.

Ruth lay down again, but got up before daylight to keep anyone from seeing who she was. Boaz said, "Don't tell anyone you were here!" Then he told her to spread out her cape. He filled it with a lot of grain and placed it on her shoulder.

When Ruth got back to town, Naomi asked her* what had happened, and Ruth told her everything. She also said, "Boaz gave me this grain, because he didn't want me to come back without something for you."

Naomi replied, "Just be patient and don't worry about what will happen. He won't stop until everything is settled today!"

Ruth and Boaz Get Married

(Ruth 4.1-22)

In the meanwhile, Boaz had gone to the meeting place at the town gate and was sitting there when the other close relative came by. So Boaz invited him to come over and sit down, and he did. Then Boaz got ten of the town leaders and also asked them to sit down. After they had sat down, he said to the man:

Naomi has come back from Moab and is selling the land that belonged to her husband Elimelech. I am telling you about this, since you are his closest relative and have the right to buy the property. If you want it, you can buy it now. These ten men and the others standing here can be witnesses. But if you don't want the property, let me know, because I am next in line.

The man replied, "I will buy it!"

"If you do buy it from Naomi," Boaz told him, "you must also marry Ruth. Then if you have a son by her, the property will stay in the family of Ruth's first husband."

The man answered, "If that's the case, I don't want to buy it! That would make problems with the property I already own.* You may buy it yourself, because I cannot."

To make a sale legal in those days, one person would take off a sandal and give it to the other. So after the man had agreed to let Boaz buy the property, he took off one of his sandals and handed it to Boaz.

Boaz told the town leaders and everyone else:

All of you are witnesses that today I have bought from Naomi the property that belonged to Elimelech and his two sons, Chilion and Mahlon. You are also witnesses that I have agreed to marry Mahlon's widow Ruth, the Moabite woman. This will keep the property in his family's name, and he will be remembered in this town.

The town leaders and the others standing there said:

We are witnesses to this. May the LORD give your wife many children, just as he did Leah and Rachel, the wives of Jacob. May you be a rich man in the tribe of Ephrathah and an important man in Bethlehem. May the children you have by this young woman make your family as famous as the family of Perez,* the son of Tamar and Judah.

Boaz married Ruth, and the LORD blessed her with a son. After his birth, the women said to Naomi:

Praise the LORD! Today he has given you a grandson to take care of you. May the boy grow up to be famous everywhere in Israel. He will* make you happy and take care of you in your old age. His mother is your daughter-in-law, and she loves you more than seven sons of your own would love you.

Naomi loved the boy and took good care of him. The

neighborhood women named him Obed, but they called him "Naomi's Boy."

When Obed grew up he had a son named Jesse, who later became the father of King David. Here is a list of the ancestors of David: Jesse, Obed, Boaz, Salmon, Nahshon, Amminadab, Ram, Hezron, and Perez.

But King David was a famous ancestor of Jesus, who would be born a thousand years later. This was the way God chose to honor this young woman, the great-grandmother of David: God placed "Ruth of Moab" in the most royal line of all!

❖ —— Hannah —— ❖

Hannah was a woman of great courage because she was a woman of great faith. In ancient Israel it was a disgrace to be married and have no children, and this is the way it was with poor Hannah, the wife of Elkanah.

(1 Samuel 1.1-28)
Elkanah lived in Ramah,* a town in the hill country of Ephraim. His great-great-grandfather was Zuph, so Elkanah was a member of the Zuph clan of the Ephraim tribe. Elkanah's father was Jeroham, his grandfather was Elihu, and his great-grandfather was Tohu.

Elkanah had two wives,* Hannah and Peninnah. Although Peninnah had children, Hannah did not have any at all.

Once a year, Elkanah traveled from his hometown to Shiloh, where he worshiped the LORD All-Powerful and offered sacrifices. Eli was the LORD's priest there, and his two sons Hophni and Phinehas served with him as priests.*

Whenever Elkanah offered a sacrifice, he gave some

of the meat* to Peninnah and some to each of her sons and daughters. But he gave Hannah even more,* because he loved Hannah very much, even though the LORD had kept her from having children of her own.

Peninnah liked to make Hannah feel miserable about not having any children, especially when the family went to the house of the LORD* each year.

One day Elkanah was there offering a sacrifice, when Hannah began crying and refused to eat. So Elkanah asked, "Hannah, why are you crying? Why won't you eat? Why do you feel so bad? Don't I mean more to you than ten sons?"

When the sacrifice had been offered, and they had eaten the meal, Hannah got up and went to pray. Eli was sitting in his chair near the door to the place of worship. Hannah was brokenhearted and was crying, as she prayed, "LORD All-Powerful, I am your servant, but I am so miserable! Please let me have a son. I will give him to you for as long as he lives, and his hair will never be cut."*

Hannah prayed silently to the LORD for a long time. But her lips were moving, and Eli thought she was drunk. "How long are you going to stay drunk?" he asked. "Sober up!"

"Sir, please don't think badly of me," Hannah answered, "I'm not drunk, and I haven't been drinking. But I feel miserable and terribly upset. I've been praying all this time, telling the LORD about my problems."

Eli replied, "You may go home now and stop worrying. I'm sure the God of Israel will answer your prayer."

"Sir, thank you for being so kind to me," Hannah said. Then she left, and after eating something, she felt much better.

Elkanah and his family got up early the next morning and worshiped the LORD. Then they went back home to Ramah. Later the LORD blessed Elkanah and Hannah with a son. She named him Samuel because she had asked the LORD for him.*

The next time Elkanah and his family went to offer their yearly sacrifice, he took along a gift that he had promised to give to the LORD. But Hannah stayed home, because she had told Elkanah, "Samuel and I won't go until he's old enough for me to stop nursing him. Then I'll give him to the LORD, and he can stay there at Shiloh for the rest of his life."

"You know what's best," Elkanah said. "Stay here until it's time to stop nursing him. I'm sure the LORD will help you do what you have promised."*

Hannah stayed home until she stopped nursing Samuel. He was still very young, but she took him to the LORD's house in Shiloh. She brought along a three-year-old bull,* a large sack of flour, and a clay jar full of wine. Hannah and Elkanah offered the bull as a sacrifice, then brought the little boy to Eli.

"Sir," Hannah said, "a few years ago I stood here beside you and asked the LORD to give me a child. Here he is! The LORD gave me just what I asked for. Now I am giving him to the LORD, and he will be the LORD's servant for as long as he lives."

(1 Samuel 2.1-11)

Elkanah* worshiped the LORD there at Shiloh, and Hannah prayed:

> You make me strong
>   and happy, LORD.
> You rescued me.

Now I can be glad
        and laugh at my enemies.
No other god* is like you.
We're safer with you
        than on a high mountain.*
I can tell those proud people,
        "Stop boasting!
Nothing is hidden from the LORD,
        and he judges what we do."

Our LORD, you break
        the bows of warriors,
but you give strength
        to everyone who stumbles.
People who once
        had plenty to eat
must now hire themselves out
        for only a piece of bread.
But you give the hungry more
        than enough to eat.
A woman did not have a child,
        and you gave her seven,
but a woman who had many
        was left with none.
You take away life,
        and you give life.
You send people down
to the world of the dead
        and bring them back again.

Our LORD, you are the one
        who makes us rich or poor.

You put some in high positions
    and bring disgrace on others.
You lift the poor and homeless
    out of garbage dumps
and give them places of honor
    in royal palaces.

You set the world on foundations,
    and they belong to you.
You protect your loyal people,
but everyone who is wicked
    will die in the darkness.
We cannot win a victory
    by our own strength.
Our Lord, those who attack you
    will be broken in pieces
when you fight back
    with thunder from heaven.
You will judge the whole earth
and give power and strength
    to your chosen king.

Elkanah and Hannah went back home to Ramah, but the boy Samuel stayed to help Eli serve the Lord.

God heard Hannah's prayer of faith, and Samuel later grew up to be a great prophet of God.

❖ —— Abigail —— ❖

The courage of Abigail led to great happiness for her, but she faced harsh difficulties along the way—including an unhappy marriage.

(1 Samuel 25.2-42)

Nabal was a very rich man who lived in Maon. He owned three thousand sheep and a thousand goats, which he kept at Carmel.* His wife Abigail was sensible and beautiful, but he was rough and mean, and he belonged to the Caleb clan.*

One day, Nabal was in Carmel, having his servants cut the wool from his sheep. David was in the desert when he heard about it. So he sent ten men to Carmel with this message for Nabal:

> I hope that you and your family are healthy and that all is going well for you. I've heard that you are cutting the wool from your sheep.

> When your shepherds were with us in Carmel, we didn't hurt them, and nothing was ever stolen from them. Ask them, and they'll tell you the same thing.
>
> My servants are your servants, and you are like a father to me. This is a day for celebrating,* so please be kind and share some of your food with us.

David's men went to Nabal and gave him David's message, then they waited for Nabal's answer.

This is what he said:

> Just who does this David think he is? That son of Jesse is just one more slave on the run from his master, and there are too many of them around these days. What makes you think I would take my bread, my water, and the meat that I've had cooked for my

own servants* and give it to you? Besides, I don't really know that David sent you!*

The men returned to their camp and told David everything Nabal had said.

"Everybody get your swords!" David ordered.

They all strapped on their swords. Two hundred men stayed behind to guard the camp, but the other four hundred followed David.

Meanwhile, one of Nabal's servants told Abigail:

David's men were often nearby while we were taking care of the sheep in the fields. They were very good to us, they never hurt us, and nothing was ever stolen from us while they were nearby. Day and night, we were as safe with them around as we would have been inside a walled city.

David sent some messengers from the desert to wish our master well, but he yelled insults at them. He's a bully who won't listen to anyone.

Isn't there something you can do? Please think of something! Our master and his family and everyone who works for him are doomed!

Abigail worked quickly. She got together two hundred loaves of bread, two large clay jars of wine, the meat from five sheep, a large sack of roasted grain, a hundred handfuls of raisins, and two hundred handfuls of dried figs. She loaded all the food on donkeys and told her servants, "Take this on ahead, and I'll catch up with you." She didn't tell her husband Nabal what she was doing.

Abigail was riding her donkey on the path that led around the hillside, when suddenly she met David and his men coming right at her.

David had just been saying, "I sure wasted my time guarding Nabal's things in the desert and keeping them

from being stolen! I was good to him, and now he pays me
back with insults. I swear that by morning there won't be a
man or boy left from his family or his servants' families. I
pray that God will punish me* if I don't do it!"

Abigail quickly got off her donkey, bowed down in
front of David, and said:

Sir, please let me speak.* Please listen to what
I say. Don't pay any attention to that good-for-
nothing Nabal. His name means "fool," and it really
fits him!

I didn't see the men you sent, but please take

this gift of food that I've brought and share it with your followers. The LORD has kept you from taking revenge and killing innocent people in the process. But I hope your enemies and anyone else who wants to hurt you will end up like Nabal. I swear this by the living LORD and by your life.

Please forgive me if I say a little more. The LORD will always protect you and your family, because you fight for him. I pray that you won't ever do anything evil as long as you live. The LORD your God will always keep you safe when your enemies try to kill you. But he will snatch away their lives quicker than you can throw a rock from a sling.

The LORD has promised to do many good things for you, even to make you the ruler of Israel. The LORD will keep his promises to you, and now your conscience will be clear, because you won't be guilty of taking revenge and killing innocent people.

When the LORD does all those good things for you, please remember me.

David told her:

Praise to the LORD, the God of Israel! He must have sent you to meet me today. And you should also be praised. Your good sense kept me from taking revenge and killing innocent people. If you hadn't come to meet me so quickly, every man and boy in Nabal's family and in his servants' families would have been killed by morning. I swear by the living LORD God of Israel who protected you that it's the truth.

David accepted the food Abigail had brought. "Don't worry," he said. "You can go home now. I'll do what you asked."

Abigail went back home and found Nabal throwing a party fit for a king. He was very drunk and feeling good, so she didn't tell him anything that night. But when he sobered up the next morning, Abigail told him everything that had happened. Nabal had a heart attack, and he just lay in bed, still as a stone. About ten days later, the LORD took his life.

David heard that Nabal had died. "Praise to the LORD!" David said, "He has judged Nabal guilty for insulting me. The LORD kept me from doing anything wrong, and he made sure that Nabal hurt only himself with his own evil."

Abigail was still at Carmel. So David sent messengers to ask her if she would marry him.

She bowed down and said, "I would even be David's slave and wash his servants' feet." Abigail got ready quickly and went back with David's messengers. She rode on her donkey, while five of her women servants walked alongside. She and David were married as soon as she got there.

Becoming David's bride was not the end of Abigail's troubles. David had to live like a man on the run because his king, Saul of Israel, was his enemy. Besides, David constantly had to defend himself from warring nations that invaded his country. During this time Achish, king of the Philistines, befriended David, but when the Philistines refused to trust him any more David returned with his troops to his own city of Ziklag.

(1 Samuel 30.1-19)

It took David and his men three days to reach Ziklag. But while they had been away, the Amalekites had been raiding in the desert around there. The had attacked

Ziklag, burned it to the ground, and had taken away the women and children. When David and his men came to Ziklag, they saw the burned-out ruins and learned that their families had been taken captive. They started crying and kept it up until they were too weak to cry any more. David's two wives, Ahinoam and Abigail, had been taken captive with everyone else.

David was desperate. His soldiers were so bitter over what had happened to their sons and daughters that they were thinking of killing David by throwing rocks at him. But David felt the LORD God giving him strength, and he said to the priest, "Abiathar, let's ask God what to do."

Abiathar brought everything he needed to get answers from God, and he went over to David. Then David asked the LORD, "Should I go after the people who raided our town? Can I catch up with them?"

"Go after them," the LORD answered. "You will catch up with them, and you will rescue your families."

David led his six hundred men to Besor Gorge, but two hundred of them were too tired to go across. So they stayed behind, while David and the other four hundred men kept on going through the countryside.

Suddenly some of David's men found an Egyptian and took him to David. They gave the Egyptian some bread, and he ate it. Then they gave him a drink of water, some dried figs, and two handfuls of raisins. This was the first time in three days he had tasted food or water. And now he felt much better.

"Who is your master?" David asked. "And where do you come from?"

"I'm from Egypt," the young man answered. "I'm the servant of an Amalekite, but he left me here three days ago because I was sick. We had attacked towns in the desert where the Cherethites live, in the area that belongs to Judah, and in the desert where the Caleb clan lives. And we burned down Ziklag."

"Will you take me to those Amalekites?" David asked.

"Yes, I will, if you promise with God as a witness that you won't kill me or hand me over to my master."

He led David to the Amalekites. They were eating and drinking everywhere, celebrating because of what they had taken from Philistia and Judah. David attacked just before sunrise the next day and fought until sunset.* Four hundred Amalekites rode away on camels, but they were the only ones who escaped.

David rescued his two wives and everyone else the Amalekites had taken from Ziklag. No one was missing — young or old, sons or daughters. David brought back everything that had been stolen.

Abigail had endured great hardship, but her love for David and her trust in David's God kept her strong. David was kind to Abigail all her days.

❖—— **The Widow of Zarephath** ——❖

We don't even know this widow's name, but she was a woman of great courage. When faced with starvation she placed her trust in the God of Elijah the prophet.

(1 Kings 17.1-24)

Elijah was a prophet from Tishbe in Gilead.* One day, he went to King Ahab and said, "I'm a servant of the living LORD, the God of Israel. And I tell you that it won't rain until I say so. There won't even be any dew on the ground."

Later, the LORD said to Elijah, "Leave and go across the Jordan River so you can hide near Cherith Creek. You can drink water from the creek and eat the food I've told the ravens to bring you."

Elijah obeyed the LORD and went to live near Cherith Creek. Ravens brought him bread and meat twice a day, and he drank water from the creek. But after a while, it dried up because there was no rain.

The LORD told Elijah, "Go to the town of Zarephath in Sidon and live there. I've told a widow in that town to give you food."

When Elijah came near the town gate of Zarephath, he saw a widow gathering sticks for a fire. "Would you please bring me a cup of water?" he asked. As she left to get it, he asked, "Would you also bring me a piece of bread?"

The widow answered:

In the name of the living LORD your God, I swear that I don't have any bread! All I have is a handful of flour and a little olive oil. I'm on my way home now with these few sticks to cook what I have for my son and me. After that, we'll starve to death. Elijah said:

Everything will be fine. Do what you said. Go home and fix something for you and your son. But first, please make a small piece of bread and bring it to me. The LORD God of Israel has promised that your jar of flour won't run out and your bottle of oil won't dry up before he sends rain for the crops.

The widow went home and did exactly what Elijah had told her. She and Elijah and her family had enough food for a long time. The LORD kept the promise that his

prophet Elijah had made, and she did not run out of flour or oil.

Several days later, the son of the woman who owned the house* got sick. The boy kept getting worse, until finally, he died.

The woman shouted at Elijah, "What have I done to you? I thought you were God's prophet! Did you come here and let my son die to remind me that I've sinned against God?"*

"Bring me your son," Elijah said. Then he took the boy from her arms and carried him upstairs to the room where he was staying. Elijah laid the boy on his bed and prayed, "LORD God, why did you do such a terrible thing to this widow? She's letting me stay here, and now you've let her son die!" Elijah stretched himself out over the boy three times, while praying, "LORD God, bring this boy back to life!"

The LORD answered Elijah's prayer, and the boy started breathing again! Elijah picked him up and carried him downstairs. He gave the boy to his mother and said, "Look, your son is alive."

"You are God's prophet!" the woman replied. "Now I know that you really do speak for the LORD."

❖ —— Esther —— ❖

Esther means "star," and the courage of the heroine of this story shines like a bright star throughout the ages.

Queen Vashti Disobeys King Xerxes

(Esther 1.1-22)

King Xerxes* of Persia lived in his capital city of Susa* and ruled one hundred twenty-seven provinces from India to Ethiopia.*

During the third year of his rule, Xerxes gave a big dinner for all his officials and officers. The governors and leaders of the provinces were also invited, and even the commanders of the Persian and Median armies came. For one hundred eighty days he showed off his wealth and spent a lot of money to impress his guests with the greatness of his kingdom.

King Xerxes soon gave another dinner and invited

everyone in the city of Susa, no matter who they were. The eating and drinking lasted seven days in the beautiful palace gardens. The area was decorated with blue and white cotton curtains tied back with purple linen cords that ran through silver rings fastened to marble columns. Couches of gold and silver rested on pavement that had all kinds of designs made from costly bright-colored stones and marble and mother-of-pearl.

The guests drank from gold cups, and each cup had a different design. The king was generous and said to them, "Drink all you want!" Then he told his servants, "Keep their cups full."

While the men were enjoying themselves, Queen Vashti gave the women a big dinner inside the royal palace.

By the seventh day, King Xerxes was feeling happy because of so much wine. And he asked his seven personal servants, Mehuman, Biztha, Harbona, Bigtha, Abagtha, Zethar, and Carkas, to bring Queen Vashti to him. The king wanted her to wear her crown and let his people and his officials see how beautiful she was. The king's servants told Queen Vashti what he had said, but she refused to go to him, and this made him terribly angry.

The king called in the seven highest officials of Persia and Media. They were Carshena, Shethar, Admatha, Tarshish, Meres, Marsena, and Memucan. These men were very wise and understood all the laws and customs of the country, and the king always asked them what they thought about such matters.

The king said to them, "Queen Vashti refused to come to me when I sent my servants for her. What does the law say I should do about that?"

Then Memucan told the king and the officials:

Your Majesty, Queen Vashti has not only

embarrassed you, but she has insulted your officials and everyone else in all the provinces.

The women in the kingdom will hear about this, and they will refuse to respect their husbands. They will say, "If Queen Vashti doesn't obey her husband, why should we?" Before this day is over, the wives of the officials of Persia and Media will find out what Queen Vashti has done, and they will refuse to obey their husbands. They won't respect their husbands, and their husbands will be angry with them.

Your Majesty, if you agree, you should write for the Medes and Persians a law that can never be changed. This law would keep Queen Vashti from ever seeing you again. Then you could let someone who respects you be queen in her place.

When the women in your great kingdom hear about this new law, they will respect their husbands, no matter if they are rich or poor.

King Xerxes and his officials liked what Memucan had said, and he sent letters to all of his provinces. Each letter was written in the language of the province to which it was sent, and it said that husbands should have control over their wives and children.

Esther Becomes Queen

(Esther 2.1-18)

After a while, King Xerxes got over being angry. But he kept thinking about what Vashti had done and the law that he had written because of her. Then the king's personal servants said:

Your Majesty, a search must be made to find you some beautiful young women. You can select officers in every province to bring them to the place where you keep your wives in the capital city of Susa. Put your servant Hegai in charge of them since that is his job. He can see to it that they are given the proper beauty treatments. Then let the young woman who pleases you most take Vashti's place as queen.

King Xerxes liked these suggestions, and he followed them.

At this time a Jew named Mordecai was living in Susa. His father was Jair, and his grandfather Shimei was the son of Kish from the tribe of Benjamin. Kish* was one of the people that Nebuchadnezzar had taken from Jerusalem, when he took King Jeconiah of Judah to Babylonia.

Mordecai had a beautiful cousin named Esther, whose Hebrew name was Hadassah. He had raised her as his own daughter, after her father and mother died. When the king ordered the search for beautiful women, many were taken to the king's palace in Susa, and Esther was one of them.

Hegai was put in charge of all the women, and from the first day, Esther was his favorite. He began her beauty treatments at once. He also gave her plenty of food and seven special maids from the king's palace, and they had the best rooms.

Mordecai had warned Esther not to tell anyone that she was a Jew, and she obeyed him. He was anxious to see how Esther was getting along and to learn what had happened to her. So each day he would walk to the front of the court where the women lived.

The young women were given beauty treatments for one whole year. The first six months their skin was rubbed with olive oil and myrrh, and the last six months it was treated with perfumes and cosmetics. Then each of them spent the night alone with King Xerxes. When a young woman went to the king, she could wear whatever clothes or jewelry she chose from the women's living quarters. In the evening she would go to the king, and the following morning she would go to the place where his wives stayed after being with him. There a man named Shaashgaz was in charge of the king's wives. Only the ones the king wanted and asked for by name could go back to the king.

Esther was the daughter of Abihail and the cousin of Mordecai, who had adopted her after her parents died.

Xerxes had been king for seven years when Esther's turn came to go to him during Tebeth, the tenth month of the year. Everyone liked Esther. The king's personal servant Hegai was in charge of the women, and Esther trusted Hegai and asked him what she ought to take with her.

Xerxes liked Esther more than he did any of the other young women. None of them pleased him as much as she did, and right away he fell in love with her and crowned her queen in place of Vashti. In honor of Esther he gave a big dinner for his leaders and officials. Then he declared a holiday everywhere in his kingdom and gave expensive gifts.

Mordecai Saves the King's Life

(Esther 2.19-23)

When the young women were brought together again, Esther's cousin Mordecai had become a palace official. He had told Esther never to tell anyone that she was a Jew, and she obeyed him, just as she had always done.

Bigthana and Teresh were the two men who guarded King Xerxes' rooms, but they got angry with the king and decided to kill him. Mordecai found out about their plans and asked Queen Esther to tell the king what he had found out. King Xerxes learned that Mordecai's report was true, and he had the two men hanged. Then the king had all of this written down in his record book as he watched.

Haman Plans to Destroy the Jews

(Esther 3.1-15)

Later, King Xerxes promoted Haman the son of Hammadatha to the highest position in his kingdom. Haman was a descendant of Agag,* and the king had given orders for his officials at the royal gate to honor Haman by kneeling down to him. All of them obeyed except Mordecai. When the other officials asked Mordecai why he disobeyed the king's command, he said, "Because I am a Jew." They spoke to him for several days about kneeling down, but he still refused to obey. Finally, they reported this to Haman, to find out if he would let Mordecai get away with it.

Haman was furious to learn that Mordecai refused to

kneel down and honor him. And when he found out that Mordecai was a Jew, he knew that killing only Mordecai was not enough. Every Jew in the whole kingdom had to be killed.

It was now the twelfth year of the rule of King Xerxes. During Nisan,* the first month of the year, Haman said, "Find out the best time for me to do this."* The time chosen was Adar,* the twelfth month.

Haman went to the king and said:

> Your Majesty, there are some people who live all over your kingdom and won't have a thing to do with anyone else. They have customs that are different from ours, and they refuse to obey your laws. We would be better off to get rid of them! Why not give orders for all of them to be killed? I can promise that you will get tons of silver for your treasury.

The king handed his official ring to Haman, who hated the Jews, and the king told him, "Do what you want with those people! You can keep their money."

On the thirteenth day of Nisan, Haman called in the king's secretaries and ordered them to write letters in every language used in the kingdom. The letters were written in the name of the king and sealed by using the king's own ring.* At once they were sent to the king's highest officials, the governors of each province, and the leaders of the different nations in the kingdom of Xerxes.

The letters were taken by messengers to every part of the kingdom, and this is what was in the letters:

On the thirteenth day of Adar, the twelfth month, all Jewish men, women, and children are to be killed. And their property is to be taken.

King Xerxes gave orders for these letters to be posted where they could be seen by everyone all over the kingdom. The king's command was obeyed, and one of the letters was read aloud to the people in the walled city of Susa. Then the king and Haman sat down to drink together, but no one in the city* could figure out what was going on.

Mordecai Asks for Esther's Help

(Esther 4.1-17)

When Mordecai heard about the letter, he tore his clothes in sorrow. Then he put on sackcloth, covered his head with ashes, and went through the city, crying and weeping. But he could go only as far as the palace gate, because no one wearing sackcloth was allowed inside the palace. In every province where the king's orders were read, the Jews cried and mourned, and they went without eating.* Many of them even put on sackcloth and sat in ashes.

When Esther's servant girls and her other servants told her what Mordecai was doing, she became very upset and sent Mordecai some clothes to wear in place of the sackcloth. But he refused to take them.

Esther had a servant named Hathach, who had been given to her by the king. She called him in and said, "Find out what's wrong with Mordecai and why he's acting this way."

Hathach went to Mordecai in the city square in front

of the palace gate, and Mordecai told him everything that had happened. He also told him how much money Haman had promised to add to the king's treasury, if all the Jews were killed.

Mordecai gave Hathach a copy of the orders for the murder of the Jews and told him that these had been read in Susa. He said, "Show this to Esther and explain what it means. Ask her to go to the king and beg him to have pity on her people, the Jews!"

Hathach went back to Esther and told her what Mordecai had said. She answered, "Tell Mordecai there is a law about going in to see the king, and all his officials and his people know about this law. Anyone who goes in to see the king without being invited by him will be put to death. The only thing that can save anyone is for the king to hold out the gold scepter to that person. And it's been thirty days since he has asked for me."

When Mordecai was told what Esther had said, he sent back this reply, "Don't think that you will escape being killed with the rest of the Jews, just because you live in the king's palace. If you don't speak up now, we will somehow get help, but you and your family will be killed. It could be that you were made queen just for a time like this!"

Esther sent a message to Mordecai, "Bring together all the Jews in Susa and tell them to go without eating for my sake! Don't eat or drink for three days and nights. My servant girls and I will do the same. Then I will go in to see the king, even if it means I must die!" Mordecai did everything Esther told him to do.

Esther Invites the King and Haman to a Dinner

(Esther 5.1-8)

Three days later, Esther dressed in her royal robes and went to the inner court of the palace in front of the throne. The king was sitting there, facing the open doorway. He was happy to see Esther, and he held out the gold scepter to her.

When Esther came up and touched the tip of the scepter, the king said, "Esther, what brings you here? Just ask, and I will give you as much as half of my kingdom."

Esther answered, "Your Majesty, please come with Haman to a dinner I will prepare for you later today."

The king said to his servants, "Hurry and get Haman, so we can accept Esther's invitation."

The king and Haman went to Esther's dinner, and while they were drinking wine, the king asked her, "What can I do for you? Just ask, and I will give you as much as half of my kingdom."

Esther replied, "Your Majesty, if you really care for me and are willing to do what I want, please come again tomorrow with Haman to the dinner I will prepare for you. At that time I will answer Your Majesty's question."

Haman Plans to Kill Mordecai

(Esther 5.9-14)

Haman was feeling great as he left. But when he saw Mordecai at the palace gate, he noticed that Mordecai did not stand up or show him any respect. This made Haman really angry, but he did not say a thing.

When Haman got home, he called together his

friends and his wife Zeresh and started bragging about his great wealth and all his sons. He told them the many ways that the king had honored him and how all the other officials and leaders had to respect him. Haman added, "That's not all! Besides the king himself, I'm the only person Queen Esther invited for dinner. She has also invited the king and me to dinner tomorrow. But none of this makes me happy, as long as I see that Jew Mordecai sitting at the palace gate."

Haman's wife and friends said to him, "Have a tower built about seventy-five feet high, and tomorrow morning ask the king to hang Mordecai there! Then later, you can have dinner with the king and enjoy yourself." This seemed like a good idea to Haman, and he had the tower built.

The King Honors Mordecai

(Esther 6.1-14)

That night the king could not sleep, and he had a servant read him the records of what had happened since he had been king. When the servant read how Mordecai had kept Bigthana and Teresh from killing the king, the king asked, "What has been done to reward Mordecai for this?"

"Nothing, Your Majesty!" the king's servants replied.

About this time, Haman came in to ask the king to have Mordecai hanged on the tower he had built. The king saw him and said, "Who is that man waiting in front of the throne room?"

The king's servants answered, "Your Majesty, it is Haman."

"Have him come in," the king commanded.

When Haman entered the room, the king asked him, "What should I do for a man I want to honor?"

Haman was sure that he was the one the king wanted to honor. So he replied, "Your Majesty, if you wish to honor a man, have someone bring him one of your own robes and one of your own horses with a fancy headdress. Have one of your highest officials place your robe on this man, and let him be led through the streets on your horse, while someone shouts, 'This is how the king honors a man!'"

The king replied, "Hurry and do just what you have said! Don't forget a thing. Get the robe and the horse for Mordecai the Jew, who is on duty at the palace gate!"

Haman got the king's robe and put it on Mordecai. He led him through the city on the horse and shouted as he went, "This is how the king honors a man!"

Afterwards, Mordecai returned to his duties at the palace gate, and Haman hurried home, hiding his face in shame. Haman told his wife and friends what had happened. Then his wife and his advisers said, "If Mordecai is a Jew, this is just the beginning of your troubles! You will end up a ruined man." They were still talking, when the king's servants came and quickly took Haman to the dinner that Esther had prepared.

Haman Is Punished

(Esther 7.1-10)

The king and Haman were dining with Esther and drinking wine during the second dinner, when the king again said, "Esther, what can I do for you? Just ask, and I will give you as much as half of my kingdom!"

Esther answered, "Your Majesty, if you really care for me and are willing to help, you can save me and my people!

That is what I really want, because a reward has been promised to anyone who kills my people. Your Majesty, if we were merely going to be sold as slaves, I would not have bothered you."*

"Who would dare to do such a thing?" the king asked.

Esther replied, "That evil Haman is the one out to get us!" Haman was terrified, as he looked at the king and the queen.

The king was so angry that he got up, left his wine, and went out into the palace garden.

Haman realized that the king had already decided what to do with him, and he stayed and begged Esther to save his life.

Just as the king came back into the room, Haman stumbled and fell on Esther, who was lying on the couch. The king shouted, "Now you're even trying to abuse my queen here in my own palace!"

As soon as the king said this, his servants covered Haman's head. Then Harbona, one of the king's personal servants, said, "Your Majesty, Haman built a tower seventy-five feet high beside his house, so he could hang Mordecai on it. And Mordecai is the very one who spoke up and saved your life."

"Hang Haman from his own tower!" the king commanded. Right away, Haman was hanged on the tower he had built to hang Mordecai, and the king calmed down.

A Happy Ending for the Jews

(Esther 8.1-2)

Before the end of the day, King Xerxes gave Esther everything that had belonged to Haman, the enemy of the Jews. Esther told the king that Mordecai was her cousin. So the king made Mordecai one of his highest officials and gave him the royal ring that Haman had worn. Then Esther put Mordecai in charge of Haman's property.

Esther's great courage had saved the day for Mordecai and her people.

❖ —— The Virgin Mary —— ❖

In the days after the prophet Malachi, there were no more messages from God for four hundred years. Then God's angel Gabriel visited Zechariah the priest, husband of Elizabeth. Gabriel told Zechariah that his wife would soon have a son who would be a great prophet. We now know that this new prophet was to be John the Baptist.

(Luke 1.26-56)

One month later God sent the angel Gabriel to the town of Nazareth in Galilee with a message for a virgin named Mary. She was engaged to Joseph from the family of King David. The angel greeted Mary and said, "You are truly blessed! The Lord is with you."

Mary was confused by the angel's words and wondered what they meant. Then the angel told Mary, "Don't be afraid! God is pleased with you, and you will have a son. His name will be Jesus. He will be great and will be called the Son of God Most

High. The Lord God will make him king, as his ancestor David was. He will rule the people of Israel forever, and his kingdom will never end."

Mary asked the angel, "How can this happen? I am not married!"

The angel answered, "The Holy Spirit will come down to you, and God's power will come over you. So your child will be called the holy Son of God. Your relative Elizabeth is also going to have a son, even though she is old. No one thought she could ever have a baby, but in three months she will have a son. Nothing is impossible for God!"

Mary said, "I am the Lord's servant! Let it happen as you have said." And the angel left her.

Mary Visits Elizabeth

A short time later Mary hurried to a town in the hill country of Judea. She went into Zechariah's home, where she greeted Elizabeth. When Elizabeth heard Mary's greeting, her baby moved within her.

The Holy Spirit came upon Elizabeth. Then in a loud voice she said to Mary:

God has blessed you more than any other woman! He has also blessed the child you will have. Why should the mother of my Lord come to me? As soon as I heard your greeting, my baby became happy and moved within me. The Lord has blessed you because you believed that he will keep his promise.

Mary's Song of Praise

Mary said:

> With all my heart
>> I praise the Lord,
>
> and I am glad
>> because of God my Savior.
>
> He cares for me,
>> his humble servant.
>
> From now on,
> all people will say
>> God has blessed me.
>
> God All-Powerful has done
> great things for me,
>> and his name is holy.
>
> He always shows mercy
> to everyone
>> who worships him.
>
> The Lord has used
>> his powerful arm
> to scatter those
>> who are proud.
>
> He drags strong rulers
>> from their thrones
> and puts humble people
>> in places of power.
>
> He gives the hungry
>> good things to eat,
> and he sends the rich away
>> with nothing in their hands.
>
> He helps his servant Israel
> and is always merciful
>> to his people.

He made this promise
to our ancestors,
to Abraham and his family
forever!

Mary stayed with Elizabeth about three months. Then she went back home.

After John was born, the promise Gabriel had given to Mary also came true.

(Luke 2.1-21)

About that time Emperor Augustus gave orders for the names of all the people to be listed in record books.* These first records were made when Quirinius was governor of Syria.*

Everyone had to go to their own hometown to be listed. So Joseph had to leave Nazareth in Galilee and go to Bethlehem in Judea. Long ago Bethlehem had been King David's hometown, and Joseph went there because he was from David's family.

Mary was engaged to Joseph and traveled with him to Bethlehem. She was soon going to have a baby, and while they were there, she gave birth to her first-born* son. She dressed him in baby clothes* and laid him in a feed box, because there was no room for them in the inn.

The Shepherds

That night in the fields near Bethlehem some shepherds were guarding their sheep. All at once an angel came down to them from the Lord, and the brightness of the Lord's glory flashed around them. The shepherds were frightened. But the angel said, "Don't be afraid! I have good news for you, which will make everyone happy. This very day in King David's hometown a Savior was born for you.

He is Christ the Lord. You will know who he is, because you will find him dressed in baby clothes and lying in a feed box."

Suddenly many other angels came down from heaven and joined in praising God. They said:

"Praise God in heaven!

Peace on earth to everyone

who pleases God."

After the angels had left and gone back to heaven, the shepherds said to each other, "Let's go to Bethlehem and see what the Lord has told us about." They hurried off and found Mary and Joseph, and they saw the baby lying in the feed box.

When the shepherds saw Jesus, they told his parents what the angel had said about him. Everyone listened and was surprised. But Mary kept thinking about all this and wondering what it meant.

As the shepherds returned to their sheep, they were praising God and saying wonderful things about him. Everything they had seen and heard was just as the angel had said.

Eight days later Jesus' parents did for him what the Law of Moses commands.* And they named him Jesus, just as the angel had told Mary when he promised she would have a baby.

The Wise Men

(Matthew 2.1-23)

When Jesus was born in the village of Bethlehem in Judea, Herod was king. During this time some wise men* from the east came to Jerusalem and said, "Where is the child born to be king of the Jews? We saw his star in the east* and have come to worship him."

When King Herod heard about this, he was worried, and so was everyone else in Jerusalem. Herod brought together all the chief priests and the teachers of the Law of Moses and asked them, "Where will the Messiah be born?"

They told him, "He will be born in Bethlehem, just as the prophet wrote,

> 'Bethlehem in the land
>   of Judea,
> you are very important
>   among the towns of Judea.
> From your town
>   will come a leader,
> who will be like a shepherd
>   for my people Israel.'"

Herod secretly called in the wise men and asked them when they had first seen the star. He told them, "Go to Bethlehem and search carefully for the child. As soon as you find him, let me know. I want to go and worship him too."

The wise men listened to what the king said and then left. And the star they had seen in the east went on ahead of them until it stopped over the place where the child was. They were thrilled and excited to see the star.

When the men went into the house and saw the child with Mary, his mother, they kneeled down and worshiped him. They took out their gifts of gold, frankincense, and myrrh* and gave them to him. Later they were warned in a dream not to return to Herod, and they went back home by another road.

The Escape to Egypt

After the wise men had gone, an angel from the Lord appeared to Joseph in a dream. The angel said, "Get up! Hurry and take the child and his mother to Egypt! Stay there until I tell you to return, because Herod is looking for the child and wants to kill him."

That night Joseph got up and took his wife and the child to Egypt, where they stayed until Herod died. So the Lord's promise came true, just as the prophet had said, "I called my son out of Egypt."

The Killing of the Children

When Herod found out that the wise men from the east had tricked him, he was very angry. He gave orders for his men to kill all the boys who lived in or near Bethlehem and were two years old and younger.

So the Lord's promise came true, just as the prophet Jeremiah had said,

"In Ramah a voice was heard
          crying and weeping loudly.
Rachel was mourning
          for her children,
and she refused
to be comforted,
          because they were dead."

The Return from Egypt

After King Herod died, an angel from the Lord appeared in a dream to Joseph while he was still in Egypt. The angel said, "Get up and take the child and his mother back to Israel. The people who wanted to kill him are now dead."

Joseph got up and left with them for Israel. But when he heard that Herod's son Archelaus was now ruler of Judea, he was afraid to go there. Then in a dream he was told to go to Galilee, and they went to live there in the town of Nazareth. So the Lord's promise came true, just as the prophet had said, "He will be called a Nazarene."*

The Boy Jesus in the Temple

(Luke 2.41-52)

Every year Jesus' parents went to Jerusalem for Passover. And when Jesus was twelve years old, they all went there as usual for the celebration. After Passover his parents left, but they did not know that Jesus had stayed on in the city. They thought he was traveling with some other people, and they went a whole day before they started looking for him. When they could not find him with their relatives and friends, they went back to Jerusalem and started looking for him there.

Three days later they found Jesus sitting in the temple, listening to the teachers and asking them questions. Everyone who heard him was surprised at how much he knew and at the answers he gave.

When his parents found him, they were amazed. His mother said, "Son, why have you done this to us? Your father and I have been very worried, and we have been searching for you!"

Jesus answered, "Why did you have to look for me? Didn't you know that I would be in my Father's house?"* But they did not understand what he meant.

Jesus went back to Nazareth with his parents and obeyed them. His mother kept on thinking about all that had happened.

Jesus became wise, and he grew strong. God was pleased with him and so were the people.

Some time afterward Jesus was baptized by John the Baptist. Then Satan tempted Jesus for forty days. When he had overcome Satan in this test, Jesus called his disciples into service with him.

(John 2.1-12)

Three days later Mary, the mother of Jesus, was at a wedding feast in the village of Cana in Galilee. Jesus and his disciples had also been invited and were there.

When the wine was all gone, Mary said to Jesus, "They don't have any more wine."

Jesus replied, "Mother, my time has not yet come!* You must not tell me what to do."

Mary then said to the servants, "Do whatever Jesus tells you to do."

At the feast there were six stone water jars that were used by the people for washing themselves in the way that their religion said they must. Each jar held about twenty or thirty gallons. Jesus told the servants to fill them to the top with water. Then after the jars had been filled, he said, "Now take some water and give it to the man in charge of the feast."

The servants did as Jesus told them, and the man in charge drank some of the water that had now turned into wine. He did not know where the wine had come from, but

the servants did. He called the bridegroom over and said, "The best wine is always served first. Then after the guests have had plenty, the other wine is served. But you have kept the best until last!"

This was Jesus' first miracle,* and he did it in the village of Cana in Galilee. There Jesus showed his glory, and his disciples put their faith in him. After this, he went with his mother, his brothers, and his disciples to the town of Capernaum, where they stayed for a few days.

Mary was not surprised by Jesus' miracle. But she now began to realize that she, too, must become her Son's disciple.

(Mark 3.31-35)

Jesus' mother and brothers came and stood outside. Then they sent someone with a message for him to come out to them. The crowd that was sitting around Jesus told him, "Your mother and your brothers and sisters* are outside and want to see you."

Jesus asked, "Who is my mother and who are my brothers?" Then he looked at the people sitting around him and said, "Here are my mother and my brothers. Anyone who obeys God is my brother or sister or mother."

Mary now gladly accepted her place among Jesus' followers, although she never ceased to hold a special place in the love of her great Son. Mary realized this in a most beautiful way on the day Jesus died to pay the penalty for our sins.

(John 19.25-27)

Jesus' mother stood beside his cross with her sister and Mary the wife of Clopas. Mary Magdalene was standing there too.* When Jesus saw his mother and his favorite disciple with her, he said to his mother, "This man is now your son." Then he said to the disciple, "She is now your mother." From then on, that disciple took her into his own home.

Ever after that day Mary would be seen among those who were the disciples of Jesus—of the Son who had come into the world through her.

(Acts 1.12-14)

The Mount of Olives was about half a mile from Jerusalem. The apostles who had gone there were Peter, John, James, Andrew, Philip, Thomas, Bartholomew, Matthew, James the son of Alphaeus, Simon, known as the Eager One,* and Judas the son of James.

After the apostles returned to the city, they went upstairs to the room where they had been staying.

The apostles often met together and prayed with a single purpose in mind.* The women and Mary the mother of Jesus would meet with them, and so would his brothers.

❖——— Elizabeth ———❖

People had always looked down on childless couples in Israel, and Zechariah and Elizabeth had grown old without children. But then a marvelous thing happened to them.

(Luke 1.5-25)

When Herod was king of Judea, there was a priest by the name of Zechariah from the priestly group of Abijah. His wife Elizabeth was from the family of Aaron.* Both of them were good people and pleased the Lord God by obeying all that he had commanded. But they did not have children. Elizabeth could not have any, and both Zechariah and Elizabeth were already old.

One day Zechariah's group of priests were on duty, and he was serving God as a priest. According to the custom of the priests, he had been chosen to go into the Lord's temple that day and to burn incense,* while the people stood outside praying.

All at once an angel from the Lord came and appeared to Zechariah at the right side of the altar. Zechariah was confused and afraid when he saw the angel. But the angel told him:

Don't be afraid, Zechariah! God has heard your prayers. Your wife Elizabeth will have a son, and you must name him John. His birth will make you very happy, and many people will be glad. Your son will be a great servant of the Lord. He must never drink wine or beer, and the power of the Holy Spirit will be with him from the time he is born.

John will lead many people in Israel to turn back to the Lord their God. He will go ahead of the Lord with the same power and spirit that Elijah* had. And because of John, parents will be more thoughtful of their children. And people who now disobey God will begin to think as they ought to. That is how John will get people ready for the Lord.

Zechariah said to the angel, "How will I know this is going to happen? My wife and I are both very old."

The angel answered, "I am Gabriel, God's servant, and I was sent to tell you this good news. You have not believed what I have said. So you will not be able to say a thing until all this happens. But everything will take place when it is supposed to."

The crowd was waiting for Zechariah and kept wondering why he was staying so long in the temple. When he did come out, he could not speak, and they knew he had seen a vision. He motioned to them with his hands, but did not say a thing.

When Zechariah's time of service in the temple was over, he went home. Soon after that, his wife was expecting a baby, and for five months she did not leave the house. She said to herself, "What the Lord has done for me will keep people from looking down on me."*

Elizabeth's cousin, Mary, lived in Nazareth. The great angel Gabriel now announced to Mary that she also would have an even greater Son than John.

(Luke 1.39-45)

A short time later Mary hurried to a town in the hill country of Judea. She went into Zechariah's home, where she greeted Elizabeth. When Elizabeth heard Mary's greeting, her baby moved within her.

The Holy Spirit came upon Elizabeth. Then in a loud voice she said to Mary:

God has blessed you more than any other woman! He has also blessed the child you will have. Why should the mother of my Lord come to me? As soon as I heard your greeting, my baby became happy and moved within me. The Lord has blessed you because you believed that he will keep his promise.

The two cousins together shared their great joy in what God was doing in their lives, and the future mother of Jesus sang a beautiful hymn of thanksgiving to God.

(Luke 1.56-80)

Mary stayed with Elizabeth about three months. Then she went back home.

The Birth of John the Baptist

When Elizabeth's son was born, her neighbors and relatives heard how kind the Lord had been to her, and they too were glad.

Eight days later they did for the child what the Law of Moses commands.* They were going to name him Zechariah, after his father. But Elizabeth said, "No! His name is John."

The people argued, "No one in your family has ever been named John." So they motioned to Zechariah to find out what he wanted to name his son.

Zechariah asked for a writing tablet. Then he wrote, "His name is John." Everyone was amazed. Right away Zechariah started speaking and praising God.

All the neighbors were frightened because of what had happened, and everywhere in the hill country people kept talking about these things. Everyone who heard about this wondered what this child would grow up to be. They knew that the Lord was with him.

Zechariah Praises the Lord

The Holy Spirit came upon Zechariah, and he began to speak:

> Praise the Lord,
> > the God of Israel!
> He has come
> > to save his people.
> Our God has given us
> > a mighty Savior*
> from the family
> > of David his servant.
> Long ago the Lord promised
> by the words
> > of his holy prophets

to save us from our enemies
and from everyone
        who hates us.
God said he would be kind
to our people and keep
        his sacred promise.
He told our ancestor Abraham
that he would rescue us
        from our enemies.
Then we could serve him
        without fear,
by being holy and good
        as long as we live.

You, my son, will be called
a prophet of God
        in heaven above.
You will go ahead of the Lord
to get everything ready
        for him.
You will tell his people
        that they can be saved
when their sins
        are forgiven.
God's love and kindness
        will shine upon us
like the sun that rises
        in the sky.*
On us who live
in the dark shadow
        of death
this light will shine
to guide us
        into a life of peace.

As John grew up, God's Spirit gave him great power. John lived in the desert until the time he was sent to the people of Israel.

❖—— A Woman with Bleeding ——❖

This nameless woman's action will always be remembered among the examples of courageous faith during Jesus' ministry.

(Luke 8.42c-48)

While Jesus was on his way, people were crowding all around him. In the crowd was a woman who had been bleeding for twelve years. She had spent everything she had on doctors,* but none of them could make her well.

As soon as she came up behind Jesus and barely touched his clothes, her bleeding stopped.

"Who touched me?" Jesus asked.

While everyone was denying it, Peter said, "Master, people are crowding all around and pushing you from every side."*

But Jesus answered, "Someone touched me, because I felt power going out from me." The woman knew that she could not hide, so she came trembling and kneeled down in front of Jesus. She told everyone why she had touched him and that she had been healed right away.

Jesus said to the woman, "You are now well because of your faith. May God give you peace!"

❖—— A Woman of Phoenicia ——❖

People who were not Jews needed great courage to ask anything of Jesus, because Jews of that time didn't usually

share their blessings with Gentiles. But this didn't stop Jesus from doing good to all who came to him.

(Mark 7.24-30)

Jesus left and went to the region near the city of Tyre, where he stayed in someone's home. He did not want people to know he was there, but they found out anyway. A woman whose daughter had an evil spirit in her heard where Jesus was. And right away she came and kneeled down at his feet. The woman was Greek and had been born in the part of Syria known as Phoenicia. She begged Jesus to force the demon out of her daughter. But Jesus said, "The children must first be fed! It isn't right to take away their food and feed it to dogs."*

The woman replied, "Lord, even dogs eat the crumbs that children drop from the table."

Jesus answered, "That's true! You may go now. The demon has left your daughter." When the woman got back home, she found her child lying on the bed. The demon had gone.

Mary Magdalene

One of the most famous of Jesus' early disciples is Mary Magdalene. As we meet her, Jesus has just forgiven the sins of a woman who came to him and washed his feet with her tears.

(Luke 8.1-3)

Soon after this, Jesus was going through towns and villages, telling the good news about God's kingdom. His twelve apostles were with him, and so were some women who had been healed of evil spirits and all sorts of diseases. One of the women was Mary Magdalene,* who once had seven demons in her. Joanna, Susanna, and many others had also used what they owned to help Jesus* and his disciples. Joanna's husband Chuza was one of Herod's officials.*

Mary Magdalene continued to be a faithful disciple of Jesus throughout the rest of her days. We see this Mary again when Jesus was crucified. Jesus' mother Mary and her sister, along with others, were standing near the cross when Jesus died.

(Matthew 27.55-61)

Many women were looking on from a distance. They had come with Jesus from Galilee to be of help to him. Mary Magdalene, Mary the mother of James and Joseph, and the mother of James and John* were some of these women.

Jesus Is Buried

That evening a rich disciple named Joseph from the town of Arimathea went and asked for Jesus' body. Pilate gave orders for it to be given to Joseph, who took the body and wrapped it in a clean linen cloth. Then Joseph put the body in his own tomb that had been cut into solid rock* and had never been used. He rolled a big stone against the entrance to the tomb and went away.

All this time Mary Magdalene and the other Mary were sitting across from the tomb.

But Mary Magdalene's grief would turn to joy a few days later.

(John 20.1-18)

On Sunday morning while it was still dark, Mary Magdalene went to the tomb and saw that the stone had been rolled away from the entrance. She ran to Simon Peter and to Jesus' favorite disciple and said, "They have taken the Lord from the tomb! We don't know where they have put him."

Peter and the other disciple started for the tomb.

They ran side by side, until the other disciple ran faster than Peter and got there first. He bent over and saw the strips of linen cloth lying inside the tomb, but he did not go in.

When Simon Peter got there, he went into the tomb and saw the strips of cloth. He also saw the piece of cloth that had been used to cover Jesus' face. It was rolled up and in a place by itself. The disciple who got there first then went into the tomb, and when he saw it, he believed. At that time Peter and the other disciple did not know that the Scriptures said Jesus would rise to life. So the two of them went back to the other disciples.

Jesus Appears to Mary Magdalene

Mary Magdalene stood crying outside the tomb. She was still weeping, when she stooped down and saw two angels inside. They were dressed in white and were sitting where Jesus' body had been. One was at the head and the other was at the foot. The angels asked Mary, "Why are you crying?"

She answered, "They have taken away my Lord's body! I don't know where they have put him."

As soon as Mary said this, she turned around and saw Jesus standing there. But she did not know who he was. Jesus asked her, "Why are you crying? Who are you looking for?"

She thought he was the gardener and said, "Sir, if you have taken his body away, please tell me, so I can go and get him."

Then Jesus said to her, "Mary!"

She turned and said to him, "Rabboni." The Aramaic word "Rabboni" means "Teacher."

Jesus told her, "Don't hold on to me! I have not yet

gone to the Father. But tell my disciples that I am going to the one who is my Father and my God, as well as your Father and your God." Mary Magdalene then went and told the disciples that she had seen the Lord. She also told them what he had said to her.

❖ ── Mary and Martha of Bethany ── ❖

Jesus' life on earth was not "all work." There were also quiet times of relaxation among friends.

(Luke 10.38-42)

The Lord and his disciples were traveling along and came to a village. When they got there, a woman named Martha welcomed him into her home. She had a sister named Mary, who sat down in front of the Lord and was listening to what he said. Martha was worried about all

that had to be done. Finally, she went to Jesus and said, "Lord, doesn't it bother you that my sister has left me to do all the work by myself? Tell her to come and help me!"

The Lord answered, "Martha, Martha! You are worried and upset about so many things, but only one thing is necessary. Mary has chosen what is best, and it will not be taken away from her."

We notice Mary and Martha again at a time of trouble in their lives. They were living near Jerusalem in the village of Bethany with Lazarus their brother.

(John 11.3-44)

The sisters sent a message to the Lord and told him that his good friend Lazarus was sick.

When Jesus heard this, he said, "His sickness won't end in death. It will bring glory to God and his Son."

Jesus loved Martha and her sister and brother. But he stayed where he was for two more days. Then he said to his disciples, "Now we'll go back to Judea."

"Teacher," they said, "the people there want to stone you to death! Why do you want to go back?"

Jesus answered, "Aren't there twelve hours in each day? If you walk during the day, you will have light from the sun, and you won't stumble. But if you walk during the night, you will stumble, because there isn't any light inside you." Then he told them, "Our friend Lazarus is asleep, and I am going there to wake him up."

They replied, "Lord, if he is asleep, he will get better." Jesus really meant that Lazarus was dead, but they thought he was talking only about sleep.

Then Jesus told them plainly, "Lazarus is dead! I am glad that I wasn't there, because now you will have a chance to put your faith in me. Let's go to him."

Thomas, whose nickname was "Twin," said to the other disciples, "Come on. Let's go so we can die with him."

Jesus Brings Lazarus to Life

When Jesus got to Bethany, he found that Lazarus had already been in the tomb four days. Bethany was only about two miles from Jerusalem, and many people had come from the city to comfort Martha and Mary because their brother had died.

When Martha heard that Jesus had arrived, she went out to meet him, but Mary stayed in the house. Martha said to Jesus, "Lord, if you had been here, my brother would not have died. Yet even now I know that God will do anything you ask."

Jesus told her, "Your brother will live again!"

Martha answered, "I know that he will be raised to life on the last day,* when all the dead are raised."

Jesus then said, "I am the one who raises the dead to life! Everyone who has faith in me will live, even if they die. And everyone who lives because of faith in me will never die. Do you believe this?"

"Yes, Lord!" she replied. "I believe that you are Christ, the Son of God. You are the one we hoped would come into the world."

After Martha said this, she went and privately said to her sister Mary, "The Teacher is here, and he wants to see you." As soon as Mary heard this, she got up and went out to Jesus. He was still outside the village where Martha had gone to meet him. Many people had come to comfort Mary, and when they saw her quickly leave the house, they thought she was going out to the tomb to cry. So they followed her.

Mary went to where Jesus was. Then as soon as she

saw him, she kneeled at his feet and said, "Lord, if you had been here, my brother would not have died."

When Jesus saw that Mary and the people with her were crying, he was terribly upset and asked, "Where have you put his body?"

They replied, "Lord, come and you will see."

Jesus started crying, and the people said, "See how much he loved Lazarus."

Some of them said, "He gives sight to the blind. Why couldn't he have kept Lazarus from dying?"

Jesus was still terribly upset. So he went to the tomb, which was a cave with a stone rolled against the entrance. Then he told the people to roll the stone away. But Martha said, "Lord, you know that Lazarus has been dead four days, and there will be a bad smell."

Jesus replied, "Didn't I tell you that if you had faith, you would see the glory of God?"

After the stone had been rolled aside, Jesus looked up toward heaven and prayed, "Father, I thank you for answering my prayer. I know that you always answer my prayers. But I said this, so that the people here would believe that you sent me."

When Jesus had finished praying, he shouted, "Lazarus, come out!" The man who had been dead came out. His hands and feet were wrapped with strips of burial cloth, and a cloth covered his face.

Jesus then told the people, "Untie him and let him go."

After this Jesus would be a welcome guest at the house of Mary and Martha whenever he came to Bethany.

❖ —— A Widow Who Gave All ——❖

It takes courage to trust God instead of clinging to our money and possessions. Here's a woman who had that kind of courage.

(Mark 12.41-44)

Jesus was sitting in the temple near the offering box and watching people put in their gifts. He noticed that many rich people were giving a lot of money. Finally, a poor widow came up and put in two coins that were worth only a few pennies. Jesus told his disciples to gather around him. Then he said:

I tell you that this poor widow has put in more than all the others. Everyone else gave what they didn't need. But she is very poor and gave everything she had. Now she doesn't have a cent to live on.

❖ —— A Persistent Widow ——❖

Jesus loved to teach by telling stories that would stick in his hearers' memories. This story has to do with a woman who had the courage to keep asking for what she needed.

(Luke 18.1-8a)

Jesus told his disciples a story about how they should keep on praying and never give up:

In a town there was once a judge who didn't fear God or care about people. In that same town there was a widow who kept going to the judge and saying, "Make sure that I get fair treatment in court."

For a while the judge refused to do anything. Finally, he said to himself, "Even though I don't fear God or care about people, I will help this widow

because she keeps on bothering me. If I don't help
her, she will wear me out."

The Lord said:

Think about what that crooked judge said.
Won't God protect his chosen ones who pray to him
day and night? Won't he be concerned for them? He
will surely hurry and help them.

NOTES (*)

Page

1   **Ur in Chaldea:** Chaldea was a region at the head of the Persian Gulf. Ur was on the main trade routes from Mesopotamia to the Mediterranean Sea.

1   **Haran:** About 550 miles northwest of Ur.

3   **Abraham:** In Hebrew "Abraham" sounds like "father of many nations."

4   **Ishmael:** It was the custom for a wife who could not have children to let her husband marry one of her servant women. The children of the servant woman would belong to the first wife. Ishmael was the son of Sarah's servant Hagar (see Genesis 16.1-16).

4   **Isaac:** In Hebrew "Isaac" sounds like the word "laugh."

5   **know such happiness:** Either the joy of making love or the joy of having children.

8   **God has made me laugh:** In Hebrew "Isaac" sounds like the word "laugh."

8   **Sleep . . . mine:** It was the custom for a wife who could not have children to let her husband marry one of her slave women. The children of the slave would belong to the first wife.

9   **Ishmael:** In Hebrew "Ishmael" sounds like "God hears."

9   **The God Who Sees Me:** Or "The God I Have Seen."

9   **no longer had to nurse Isaac:** In ancient Israel mothers nursed their children until they were about three years old. Then there was a family celebration.

9   **playing:** Hebrew; one ancient translation "playing with her son Isaac."

9   **Get rid . . . son:** When Abraham accepted Ishmael as his son, it gave Ishmael the right to inherit part of what Abraham owned. But slaves who were given their freedom lost the right to inherit such property.

14 **ring in her nose:** In biblical times, nose-rings were popular jewelry items, as were earrings.

17 **old family servant woman:** Probably Deborah, who had taken care of Rebekah from the time she was born.

18 **Who Sees Me:** Or "I Have Seen."

18 **covered her face with her veil:** Since the veiling of a bride was part of the wedding ceremony, this probably means that she was willing to become the wife of Isaac.

18 **took Rebekah into the tent:** This shows that Rebekah is now the wife of Isaac and the successor of Sarah as the leading woman in the tribe.

18 **Paddan Aram:** This may be another name for the region around the city of Haran.

19 **Esau:** In Hebrew "Esau" sounds like a word that means "hairy."

19 **Jacob:** In Hebrew, one meaning of the name "Jacob" is "cheater."

22 **Jacob:** In Hebrew "Jacob" sounds like the word for "cheat."

23 **lose . . . day:** Esau would be hunted down as a murderer if he killed Jacob, and so Rebekah would lose both of her sons.

24 **Paddan Aram:** This may be another name for the region around the city of Haran.

25 **Joseph:** The son of Jacob who had been sold as a slave and taken to Egypt. Later he became an important official because he had helped the king.

25 **Pithom and Rameses:** This is the only mention of Pithom in the Bible; its exact location is unknown, though it may have been in the northern Delta of Egypt. Rameses is the famous Delta city that was the home of Pharaoh Rameses II; its exact location is also unknown.

25 **Hebrew:** An earlier term for "Israelite."

27 **Moses:** In Hebrew "Moses" sounds like a word meaning "pull out."

29 **Acacia:** Or "Shittim."

29 **woman:** Hebrew "prostitute"; Rahab may also have been an innkeeper. Strangers staying at her house would not normally have attracted much attention.

29 **flax plants:** The stalks of flax plants were harvested, soaked in water, and dried, then their fibers were separated and spun into thread, which was afterwards woven into linen cloth.

29 **gate:** In ancient times many towns and cities had walls with heavy gates that were shut at night for protection.

29 **Red Sea:** Or "Sea of Reeds."

31 **wall:** In ancient times cities and larger towns had high walls around them to protect them against attack. Sometimes houses would be built up against the wall so that the city wall formed one wall of the house. This added strength to the city wall.

32 **trumpets:** These were hollowed-out ram's horns.

33 **destroy . . . now belongs to the LORD:** Destroying a city and everything in it, including its people and animals, showed that it belonged to the LORD and could no longer be used by humans.

33 **sent:** See Joshua 2.1-21.

33 **Be careful . . . fault:** One ancient translation; Hebrew "Don't keep any of it for yourself. If you do, God will destroy both you and Israel."

34 **camp:** Rahab and her family were not Israelites. If they stayed in the Israelite army camp, God would not help the Israelite army in battle. Later on, Rahab and her family became part of Israel.

34 **the LORD's house:** A name for the place of worship, which at that time was the sacred tent.

34   **by the time . . . dead:** Or "when he puts gates into the town wall, his youngest son will die."

35   **leader:** The Hebrew text has "judge"; in Israel leaders, called "judges," not only judged legal cases, but also led the Israelites in battle and sometimes performed religious duties.

37   **the village . . . Zaanannim:** Or "the oak tree in the village of Zaanannim."

39   **villagers . . . fields:** One possible meaning for the difficult Hebrew text.

39   **Deborah:** Or "I, Deborah."

39   **The Israelites . . . attacked:** One possible meaning for the difficult Hebrew text.

40   **Anyone . . . water:** One possible meaning for the difficult Hebrew text.

40   **side:** One possible meaning for the difficult Hebrew text of verse 13.

40   **But . . . at all:** Or "But the people of Reuben couldn't make up their minds."

40   **sheep pens:** Or "campfires."

40   **No . . . come:** Or "The people of Reuben couldn't make up their minds."

41   **to attack the enemy:** One possible meaning for the difficult Hebrew text.

41   **stream . . . Megiddo:** Probably refers to one of the streams that flow into the Kishon River.

41   **stars:** In ancient times, the stars were sometimes regarded as supernatural beings.

42   **and beautiful . . . wear:** One possible meaning for the difficult Hebrew text.

43   **Moab:** The people of Moab worshiped idols and were usually enemies of the people of Israel.

44   **for you to marry:** When a married man died and left no children, it was the custom for one of his brothers to

marry his widow. Any children they had would then be thought of as those of the dead man, so that his family name would live on.

44 **Life . . . me:** Or "I'm sorry that the LORD has turned against me and made life so hard for you."

45 **even by death:** Or "by anything but death."

45 **Mara:** In Hebrew the name "Naomi" means "pleasant," and the name "Mara" means "bitter."

45 **grain left . . . workers:** It was the custom at harvest time to leave some grain in the field for the poor to pick up (see Leviticus 19.10; 23.22).

46 **she has . . . rest:** One possible meaning for the difficult Hebrew text.

48 **He:** Or "The LORD."

49 **lift the covers . . . feet:** To ask for protection and possibly for marriage.

49 **So . . . me:** To show that he would protect and take care of her.

50 **When . . . her:** Some Hebrew manuscripts and two ancient translations; most Hebrew manuscripts "Boaz went back to town. Naomi asked Ruth."

50 **property . . . own:** This property would then have to be shared with Ruth and her children as well as with his own family.

51 **Perez:** One of the sons of Judah; he was an ancestor of Boaz and of many others who lived in Bethlehem.

51 **May . . . famous . . . He will:** Or "May the LORD be praised everywhere in Israel. Your grandson will."

52 **Ramah:** The Hebrew has "Ramathaim," a longer form of "Ramah" (see verse 19).

52 **two wives:** Having more than one wife was allowed in those times.

52 **Eli . . . priests:** One ancient translation; Hebrew

"Hophni and Phinehas, the two sons of Eli, served the LORD as priests."

53 **meat:** For some sacrifices, like this one, only part of the meat was burned. Some was given to the priest, and the rest was eaten by the family and guests of the worshiper (see Leviticus 3.1-17; 7.11-18).

53 **even more:** One possible meaning for the difficult Hebrew text.

53 **house of the LORD:** Another name for the place of worship at Shiloh, which still may have been the sacred tent at this time.

53 **his hair . . . cut:** Never cutting the child's hair would be a sign that he would belong to the LORD (see Numbers 6.1-21, especially verse 5).

54 **him:** In Hebrew "Samuel" sounds something like "He who is from God" or "The name of God" or "His name is God."

54 **the LORD . . . promised:** The Dead Sea Scrolls and one ancient translation; the Standard Hebrew Text "the LORD will do what he said."

54 **a three-year-old bull:** The Dead Sea Scrolls and two ancient translations; the Standard Hebrew Text "three bulls."

54 **Elkanah:** One possible meaning for the difficult Hebrew text.

56 **god:** The Hebrew text has "holy one," a term for supernatural beings or gods.

56 **mountain:** The Hebrew text has "rock," which is sometimes used in poetry to compare the Lord to a mountain where his people can run for protection from their enemies. The translation given for this verse is one possible meaning for the difficult Hebrew text.

58 **Carmel:** About one mile north of Maon in the southern desert of Judah.

58   **belonged . . . clan:** Or "behaved like a dog."

58   **celebrating:** Cutting the wool from the sheep was a time for celebrating as well as for working.

59   **servants:** Hebrew "shearers," the servants who cut the wool from the sheep.

59   **I don't . . . sent you:** Or "I don't know where you come from."

60   **me:** Hebrew "my enemies."

60   **please . . . speak:** Or "it's my fault."

64   **just . . . sunset:** Or "at dusk, and fought until sunset on the next day."

64   **from Tishbe in Gilead:** Or "from the settlers in Gilead."

66   **the woman who owned the house:** This may or may not be the same woman as the widow in verses 8-16.

66   **Did you . . . God:** In ancient times people sometimes thought that if they sinned, something terrible would happen to them.

67   **Xerxes:** The Hebrew text has "Ahasuerus," who was better known as King Xerxes I (485-464 B.C.).

67   **in his capital city of Susa:** Or "in his royal fortress in the city of Susa." Susa was a city east of Babylon and a winter home for Persian kings.

67   **Ethiopia:** The Hebrew text has "Cush," which was a region south of Egypt that included parts of the present countries of Ethiopia and Sudan.

70   **Kish:** Or "Mordecai." The Hebrew text has "he."

72   **Agag:** Agag was a king who had fought against the Jews long before the time of Esther.

73   **Nisan:** About mid-March to mid-April.

73   **Find out . . . do this:** The Hebrew text has "cast lots," which were pieces of wood or stone used to find out how and when to do something. For "lots" the Hebrew text uses the Babylonian word "purim."

73 **Adar:** About mid-February to mid-March.

73 **king's own ring:** Melted wax was used to seal a letter, and while the wax was still soft, the king's ring was pressed in the wax to show that the letter was official.

74 **walled city . . . city:** Or "royal fortress . . . rest of the city."

74 **went without eating:** The Israelites would sometimes go without eating (also called "fasting") in times of great sorrow or danger.

80 **I would . . . bothered you:** One possible meaning for the difficult Hebrew text.

84 **names . . . listed in record books:** This was done so that everyone could be made to pay taxes to the Emperor.

84 **Quirinius was governor of Syria:** It is known that Quirinius made a record of the people in A.D. 6 or 7. But the exact date of the record taking that Luke mentions is not known.

84 **first-born:** The Jewish people said that the first-born son in each of their families belonged to the Lord.

84 **dressed him in baby clothes:** The Greek text has "wrapped him in wide strips of cloth," which was how young babies were dressed.

86 **what the Law of Moses commands:** This refers to circumcision. It is the cutting off of skin from the private part of Jewish boys eight days after birth to show that they belong to the Lord.

86 **wise men:** People famous for studying the stars.

86 **his star in the east:** Or "his star rise."

87 **frankincense, and myrrh:** Frankincense was a valuable powder that was burned to make a sweet smell. Myrrh was a valuable sweet-smelling powder often used in perfume.

90   **He will be called a Nazarene:** The prophet who said this is not known.

91   **in my Father's house:** Or "doing my Father's work."

91   **my time has not yet come!:** The time when the true glory of Jesus would be seen, and he would be recognized as God's Son. See John 12.23.

92   **miracle:** The Greek text has "sign." In the Gospel of John the word "sign" is used for the miracle itself and as a way of pointing to Jesus as the Son of God.

93   **and sisters:** These words are not in some manuscripts.

93   **Jesus' mother stood beside his cross with her sister and Mary the wife of Clopas. Mary Magdalene was standing there too:** The Greek text may also be understood to include only three women ("Jesus' mother stood beside the cross with her sister, Mary the mother of Clopas. Mary Magdalene was standing there too.") or merely two women ("Jesus' mother was standing there with her sister Mary of Clopas, that is Mary Magdalene."). "Of Clopas" may mean "daughter of" or "mother of."

94   **known as the Eager One:** The Greek text has "Cananaean," which probably comes from a Hebrew word meaning "zealous" (see Luke 6.15). "Zealot" was the name later given to the members of a Jewish group which resisted and fought against the Romans.

94   **met together and prayed with a single purpose in mind:** Or "met together in a special place for prayer."

94   **Abijah . . . Aaron:** The Jewish priests were divided into two groups, and one of these groups was named after Abijah. Each group served in the temple once a year for two weeks at a time. Aaron, the brother of Moses, was the first priest.

94   **burn incense:** This was done twice a day, once in the morning and again in the late afternoon.

95 **Elijah:** The prophet Elijah was known for his power to work miracles.

96 **keep people from looking down on me:** When a married woman could not have children, it was thought that the Lord was punishing her.

97 **what the Law of Moses commands:** This refers to circumcision. It is the cutting off of skin from the private part of Jewish boys eight days after birth to show that they belong to the Lord.

97 **a mighty Savior:** The Greek text has "a horn of salvation." In the Scriptures animal horns are often a symbol of great strength.

98 **like the sun that rises in the sky:** Or "like the Messiah coming from heaven."

99 **She had spent everything she had on doctors:** Some manuscripts do not have these words.

99 **from every side:** Some manuscripts add "and you ask, 'Who touched me?' "

100 **feed it to dogs:** The Jewish people often referred to Gentiles as dogs.

101 **Magdalene:** Meaning "from Magdala," a small town on the western shore of Lake Galilee. There is no hint that she is the sinful woman in Luke 7.36-50.

101 **used what they owned to help Jesus:** Women often helped Jewish teachers by giving them money.

101 **Herod's officials:** Herod Antipas, the son of Herod the Great.

102 **of James and John:** The Greek text has "of Zebedee's sons." See Matthew 26.37.

102 **tomb . . . solid rock:** Some of the Jewish people buried their dead in rooms carved into solid rock. A heavy stone was rolled against the entrance.

107 **the last day:** When God will judge all people.